George Grant

In Conversation

George Grant

In Conversation

DAVID CAYLEY

First published in 1995 by
House of Anansi Press Limited
1800 Steeles Avenue West
Concord, Ontario
L4K 2P3
Tel. (416) 445-3333
Fax (416) 445-5967

Canadian Cataloguing in Publication Data
Grant, George, 1918–1988
George Grant in conversation

ISBN 0-88784-553-3

1. Grant, George, 1918–1988 — Interviews.
2. Philosophy, Canadian — 20th century. 3. Political
science — Philosophy. 4. Canada — Politics and
government. 5. Nationalism — Canada. I. Cayley,
David. II. Title.

B995.G74A3 1995   191   C94-930059-4

Cover Design: Brant Cowie/ArtPlus Limited
Computer Graphics: Mary Bowness
Printed and bound in Canada

*House of Anansi Press gratefully acknowledges the support of the
Canada Council, the Ontario Ministry of Citizenship, Culture, and
Recreation, Ontario Arts Council, and Ontario Publishing Centre in
the development of writing and publishing in Canada.*

Contents

PREFACE

George Grant had a lifelong association with the CBC, and it was, in significant part, through the CBC that he was so well known and well loved by Canadians. He began his career as an organizer for CBC Radio's *Citizen's Forum* in 1943, contributing reviews and "talks," as they were then called, throughout the 1950s. In 1958 he inaugurated *University of the Air*, the program that eventually became *Ideas*, with a series of lectures that were later published as his first book, *Philosophy in the Mass Age*. He continued to be heard regularly on both radio and television during the 1960s, and in 1969 recorded the Massey Lectures, which appeared in book form as *Time as History*. Altogether, his contributions to the CBC probably exceeded those of any other Canadian thinker of his generation, except perhaps Northrop Frye.

I had the honour of making the last major presentation of Grant's ideas on CBC Radio: a three-hour series called "The Moving Image of Eternity," broadcast on *Ideas* beginning in January of 1986, less than three years before his death.[1] The programs were drawn from conversations with friends and colleagues of Grant's, and from the present interview. It was recorded during five days in August of 1985 in the Grants' living room at 1622 Walnut Street in Halifax. Grant and I had agreed that my programs would present an intellectual, not a personal, biography, and occasionally, when some personal matter arose or when he feared giving offence, he would ask to have the tape recorder turned off. (Two years earlier some unguarded remarks in an interview with Judy Steed for the *Globe and Mail* had embarrassed him and brought a stern rebuke from his older sister Charity.[2]) My questioning was guided mainly by my reading of the five books Grant had then written — *Technology and Justice*, the last, would not appear until the following year — and by my desire to present a full portrait of his thought.

At that time, there was no thought of publishing anything but a transcription of the edited programs. The opportunity to publish a book arose later, when House of Anansi Press created the "In Conversation" series in 1992 in order to publish interviews I had subsequently recorded for *Ideas*, with Ivan Illich and Northrop Frye. With this vehicle available, and the first two books in the series well received, we decided to retrieve the earlier interview with George Grant, the first I had done of a scale and comprehensiveness to warrant publication as a book.

Readers of interviews, like listeners to radio programs, must often marvel at the unlikely clarity and economy with which people express themselves. They probably soon conclude, if they think about it, that considerable cosmetic surgery is involved; and that's usually so. Speech borrows much of its grammar from the occasion of its utterance. Things that are made plain by a gesture, a look, or a shorthand allusion to what was said before the tape recorder was turned on need to be spelled out in writing. Mannerisms that please an auditor, like Grant's persistent solicitude about whether I saw what he meant, may irritate a reader. I have edited freely in the interest of an orderly and explicit text, while at the same time trying to preserve the vividness of spontaneous talk. These are Grant's words as he spoke them, but without the false starts, awkward sentence structure, and other infelicities that might interfere with a reader's enjoyment or understanding. I have added clarifying words sparingly and only when I was completely confident of the intended meaning.

I knew George Grant only during the few days that these conversations were recorded, an acqaintance far too brief to be called a friendship, but it still attached me to him very strongly. He was, as the journalist Charles Taylor has said, "a burly man of impressive corporation,"[3] and his trademark, as nearly everyone who sat with him has noted, was the cascade of cigarette ash that would tumble down his broad front as he became engrossed in conversation. I found him a touching, unguarded companion, whose intelligence

seemed deeply rooted in his heart. I was grieved when
his death in 1988 cut off my hope of seeing him again.

In his biography of George Grant, William
Christian relates a remark made by Grant's mother,
Maude, when Grant told her of his intention to study
philosophy and theology at Oxford after the war. "You
have always been the poseur of the family, George,"
she said, "but this is the worst pose of all."[4] I felt a
sense of recognition when I read this observation, and
recalled with amusement a certain staginess about
Grant even as an old man. But though a mother
should not be lightly contradicted, I think that if his
attachment to philosophy was ever a pose — and
what commitment is not at first at least partly a pose?
— it was a pose he came to inhabit so passionately and
so completely that the pose in the end was the man.
Philosophy, from its Greek roots, means the love of
wisdom, and Grant brought wisdom to bear on politics and society at a time when most doubted that
wisdom was more than a pretentious word for intellectual technique. He was, moreover, an accessible
public philosopher, easily read and easily met with
during his years as a teacher, lecturer, and writer.

"In an age where artists paint for other artists, writers write for other writers and philosophers
philosophize for other philosophers," his friend and
colleague Louis Greenspan has written, "George
Grant steadfastly addressed the public realm."[5] In
these pages, Grant can be met with again, doing what
he did while he lived: teaching philosophy. I hope this
book will provide Grant's old friends with the pleasure of hearing his resonant voice once again, and that
it will make some new friends for a body of work that

I think remains vital even in changed circumstances.

The interview was recorded by Rod Sneddon and transcribed by Hedy Muysson. I am grateful to CBC Radio, to my executive producer Bernie Lucht, to Damiano Pietropaolo who produced "The Moving Image of Eternity," to Gail Brownell who has cheerfully organized so many of my projects over the years, to all my other colleagues at *Ideas*, and to Jutta Mason for her continuing friendship and good counsel.

I have introduced the interview with a critical essay in which I outline my reading of Grant. I hope this will provide a context in which the interview can be read, particularly by those relatively unfamiliar with Grant's work.

I dedicate the work to Ivan Illich, a friend who has also thought the "madness in the modern," but in a rather different key.

INTRODUCTION

It was through the defence crisis of 1963 that George Grant first became widely known in Canada. The crisis came about when the Diefenbaker government refused to comply with the American government's demand that Canada arm missiles it had previously acquired from the United States with nuclear warheads. The Liberal Party took advantage of the government's weakness by reversing its opposition to nuclear arms for Canada. The Canadian military sided with the Americans and arranged a press conference in Ottawa where an American general was allowed to challenge the Canadian government's good faith. Diefenbaker's own Defence Minister, Douglas Harkness, resigned, and when the NDP, who then held the balance of power, sided with the Liberals, the government fell.

These were dramatic political events, but at the time, observers gave them no deeper significance than appeared on the surface. After six years of wavering leadership and self-righteous rhetoric, Diefenbaker was already something of an embarrassment to the cosmopolitan élites of urban Canada. Next to the dashing and dynamic John F. Kennedy, he looked somewhat fusty and out of date. Few seemed to object to the overt American interference in Canadian affairs. Then, in 1965, in a book called *Lament for a Nation*, George Grant offered a radically different interpretation of what had happened in Ottawa in 1963. Grant did not mitigate Diefenbaker's considerable flaws. He wrote at length about his pettiness and personal vanity, the hollowness of his populism, the incoherence of his economic policies, his prejudices against Quebec, and his undermining of the CBC. He admitted that the desertion of the "intellectual community" from Diefenbaker "was a measure of how far [Diefenbaker] had carried yahooism in his years in office."[6] (The fact that Diefenbaker later asked Grant to write his life suggests that he never actually read the book he had been told praised him.) But what was so strikingly different about Grant's book was that he treated Diefenbaker's flaws as tragic, not comic, and argued that "Diefenbaker's confusions and inconsistencies [were] essential to the Canadian fate" (5). In what others had derisively dismissed as good riddance, Grant discovered the symbolic moment at which Canada had ceased to be a distinct society. Canada, Grant argued, had been founded on its difference from the United States. It had incarnated "a greater sense of order and restraint," and "a firmer sense of the common good" (70). But these virtues, he said, could not survive the homogenizing effects of continental economic integration and rapid technological change. Diefenbaker's confused and incoherent resistance to American bullying in 1963 was the last doomed gasp of our independence.

Grant's book had a paradoxical effect. To his own generation, who had grown up during the Depression and fought in the Second World War, it made very little difference; but among the young it exerted a powerful fascination. Dennis Lee, who later became Grant's friend and editor, said that "it spoke to parts of me that I didn't know existed."[7] For those who had grown up in the suburban enclaves of postwar prosperity and who were wide open to the technological forces that Grant claimed were dissolving the loyalties which had held Canada together, *Lament for a Nation* offered a fresh and inspiring account of politics. The ringing grandeur of the book's style, the depth of feeling with which it was written, its echo of the biblical Book of Lamentations — "Jerusalem remembers in the days of her affliction and bitterness all the precious things that were hers from days of old"[8] — all hinted at a higher purpose than the children of the 1950s had previously discerned in Canada's national existence. Grant held Canada before them as a society in which the common good had meant more than the sum of individual interests, and made them feel that politics ought to be about the conservation of this good and not just the management of technological progress. His argument appealed across the political spectrum, to the organizations of the New Left and to Young

Conservative clubs alike. Grant's younger readers grasped at the very good that he claimed was disappearing, and they adopted him as their mentor.

Lament for a Nation was a seminal influence on the spirit of nationalism that emerged in Canada during the 1960s; but Grant's argument, in fact, went far beyond Canada and far beyond nationalism. His book was constructed in layers, or concentric rings, beginning with the particular circumstances of Diefenbaker's fall, and ending with a meditation on the idea that Canada's redundancy was only an instance of a more general tendency in technological civilization to extinguish all local differences. Diefenbaker served as the sign of Canada's disappearance, but nothing in the argument suggested that this was a fate he could have prevented. Continentalism had been the policy of the Liberal Party throughout the twentieth century, and by the time Franklin Delano Roosevelt formally included Canada in the embrace of the American Empire (speaking at Queen's University in 1938 Roosevelt said, "I give to you assurance that the people of the United States will not stand idly by if domination of Canadian soil is threatened by any other empire"[9]), Canada was already committed to a branch-plant economy which was steadily eroding any fundamental difference between itself and the United States. This subordination to the United States, in Grant's view, represented something more than just the domination of a weaker state by a stronger one. The United States was the world's purest expression of "progressive liberalism," and as such was the spearhead of a movement to eliminate all historical differences in favour of what he called "the universal and homogeneous state," a condition in which freedom would be universally recognized as the highest good and technology would render all places and political conditions the same. Canada was facing not just a garden-variety imperialism of the kind that many small states had withstood for centuries, but absorption into the worldwide destiny that Grant believed was best summed up in the word technology. Through the Loyalist refusal of the American Revolution in English Canada and through the Catholic Church in Quebec, Canadians had remained connected to an old conservative tradition which had been willing "to use the government to protect the common good,"[10] but conservatism in this sense had now become literally impossible: "A science that leads to the conquest of nature . . . produces such a dynamic society that it is impossible to conserve anything for long . . . Conservatives . . . not committed to a dynamic technology . . . cannot hope to make any popular appeal. [Those who] are so committed cannot hope to be conservatives" (66). "The impossibility of conservatism in our era," Grant concluded, was "the impossibility of Canada" (68).

Lament for a Nation was a dazzling rhetorical performance, and it produced an effect of exhilaration in its readers, even as it apparently left them standing in midair. It was an elegy that induced hope, an evocation of a vanished good that still seemed pregnant with some new possibility. Grant, as his biographer William Christian has written, was "a singer of enchanted songs . . . love songs,"[11] and even though his lament "cr[ied] out at the death or at the dying of something loved,"[12] it was his ability to speak in a modern context of "loving the good" that transfixed his readers. Louis Greenspan, who was a colleague of Grant's at McMaster University for many years, recalled a similar impression when he first encountered Grant in the classroom at Dalhousie in the 1950s.

> I still remember his first entrance into class. He came walking in with a rather dishevelled outfit. But then when he turned to the class he spoke with tremendous clarity, dignity, almost defiance . . . I . . . thought of him as a member of an aristocracy, most of whose members had been recently guillotined. He was the remnant.[13]

Grant reminded people of something lost, but at the same time gave them hope — both in his person and in his writings — that it might be recovered. The ultimate source of this hope in Grant's own life was a conviction that had come to him in the darkest hour of the Second World War. He had grown up within what he called "the great sane secular liberalism" that had shaped the Canada of the late nineteenth and early twentieth centuries,[14] but in the midst of the chaos of the war he had been converted. He described the experience very simply in the interview that follows: "I got off my bicycle and walked through a gate, and I believed in God. I just knew that was it for me." What he knew, he said, was that "beyond time and space there was order,"[15] and therefore we do not ultimately belong to ourselves but to God. The order of things is not one that we measure and define but one that measures and defines us.

This was the central experience of Grant's life, the pivot on which all his thinking would finally turn, but not all the consequences were immediately evident. He still had to learn, as he said, how to think about what had happened to him. In some cases the direction this thinking would take was quickly evident. As early as 1949, for instance, when he was asked to write the section on philosophy for the Massey Commission, he began his essay with a prophetic sentence that was so utterly out of tune with the prevailing academic definition of philosophy that it offended many of his senior colleagues. "The study of philosophy," he wrote, "is the analysis of the traditions of our society and the judgement of those traditions against our varying intuitions of the Perfection of God."[16] In other ways, he remained for many years within the embrace of "progressive liberalism," not yet daring to consider what he called "the great central thought that I have tried to think: that the Western experiment, the experiment that [has] gone on since the seventeenth century in both natural science and political science, [has been] a mistake."

Grant's divided mind was evident in his first book, *Philosophy in the Mass Age*, written in response to a commission from the CBC and published in 1959. When he wrote it he was already quite troubled at the seemingly relentless transformation of his world. "Even in the ten short years I have lived in Halifax," he said, "I have watched with amazement the speed with which the corporation empires have taken over the old culture and made it their own."[17] On a trip to Toronto in 1954 he wrote to his wife, Sheila, "Unless we are called to be destroyed, we must stay in Nova Scotia . . . It really is so fantastic that all I am is one screaming nerve."[18] Even in the late 1940s he was already writing to a friend that "Sheila and I are more and more thinking of becoming, with friends, farmers so that there would be some kind of communal and religious life that will survive when the real breakdown of industrial society comes"(141). And yet he could still say in *Philosophy in the Mass Age* that this destructive and possibly doomed "progress," was also overcoming scarcity and relaxing the grip of tradition and, therefore, preparing the "dawn of a new age of reason in North America" (13).

The fact that Grant had not yet made up his mind about how modernity was to be understood is by no means a fault in *Philosophy in the Mass Age*. The book actually lays out with wonderful clarity the questions that concerned Grant throughout his life. What he wanted to do, he said, was "to grasp the differing imports of ancient and modern thought" (107). He found the ancient view epitomized in the idea that there is a natural law, and that this law represents "an order in the universe which human reason can discover; and, according to which the human will must act so that it can attune itself to the universal harmony" (28). Obedience, or attunement in this account of things, is higher than freedom. Grant illustrated his point with a quotation from St. Augustine: "To be able not to sin is a great liberty; not to be able to sin is the greatest." At the height of Western civilization is Christ's statement, "Not my will but thine be done."[19] Our freedom consists only in our capacity to accept or refuse a timeless order which we did not make, which we cannot fully comprehend, and for which we cannot finally be responsible.

Against this doctrine Grant set the modern account of history as progress. He argued that "what [had] made Western culture so dynamic [was] its impregnation with the Judaeo-Christian idea that history is the divinely ordained process of man's salvation."[20] The Western church had understood the Incarnation of God in Jesus Christ as having impressed on time a providential purpose and an irreversible direction. Unlike the ancient intuition which was summed up in Plato's beautiful figure of time as the moving image of eternity, the Judaeo-Christian view allowed for genuine novelty and progress. Truth had entered time and made of history the sphere in which good would finally overcome evil. Eventually this idea of history as the realization of the Kingdom of God "pass[ed] over into the idea of history as progress, culminating in the Kingdom of Man" (49). "The mediating term between history as providence and history as progress," Grant said, "[was] the idea of freedom [or] subjectivity" (49). This idea, he thought, had begun in the Reformation with the overthrow of the church's power to interpose its dogmas, rituals, and hierarchies between the believer and God; but by the Enlightenment, European thinkers had already begun to chafe at the bonds imposed on thought by the very existence of God. Grant quoted Voltaire's essay on the earthquake at Cadiz, in which Voltaire argued that it is immoral to believe in a God who would permit such an obviously evil thing to happen. In Voltaire's view, belief in an all-powerful God who providentially orders history was an illusion fostered by clerics who claimed authority on the basis of their privileged access to an eternal order. The overcoming of evil, he thought, could only be the work of untrammelled human freedom. It depended on human beings recognizing themselves as the source of their own ideas and the authors of their own destinies and not as the slaves of some celestial tyrant. This might have been a terrifying idea, as later thinkers like Friedrich Nietzsche and Søren Kierkegaard would discover, but the Enlightenment gave it an optimistic colour, Grant said, because the overthrow of God initially took place in the context of "a civilization dominated by Christian ideas about time" (51). Christian providentialism transposed into the key of responsible human freedom led to the faith that is summed up in the word progress: that human beings have a right and duty to alleviate evil and remake the world without limit.

George Grant ended *Philosophy in the Mass Age* by bringing the contradiction between human freedom and an absolute moral order to a fine point, and then confessing his inability to effect a final reconciliation between these two views. He testified to his Christian faith:

> However . . . crazy the world may seem, doubt is not my final standpoint, because there is that which I do not doubt. In speaking of morality, I speak ultimately from the side of the law. To do so is to affirm that the idea of God ultimately regulates moral philosophy; that the moral law is an unconditional authority of which we do not take the measure, but by which we ourselves are measured. (100)

But then he said that only "a great philosopher" would be able to demonstrate how such a faith could "withstand any argument brought against it" (101). And he also acknowledged "the truth of our freedom and the truth of progress" (98), as represented in the overcoming of scarcity and servitude during modernity. This defined his dilemma. He recognized the obvious good embodied in progress, but he couldn't see how our freedom to make of the world what we want is compatible with the absolute limit inherent in the existence of God. Is a good that we make by our free choice compatible with a transcendent good that we can only discover by patiently attending on it? He knew, he said, that a certain disharmony between freedom and moral law was evident in the fact that "character and intellect are ever more in disunion" (102), but he didn't know whether the difficulty could be overcome. He said only that the problem must be thought about "in the light of the history of philosophy . . . The true relation of freedom to law can only be thought by those who have immersed themselves in the history of philosophy" (107).

When *Philosophy in the Mass Age* was reprinted in 1966 Grant added a new introduction in which he said that, in the meantime, he had made up his mind about some of the questions he had left unresolved in his lectures. At the time the book was written, he said, he had still "considered [G.W.F.] Hegel the greatest of all philosophers" and had believed that Hegel had synthesized "all that was true and beautiful and good in the Greek world . . . with Christianity and with the freedom of the Enlightenment and with modern science."[21] Under Hegel's spell he had believed that what was lost in the pursuit of technological mastery could be regained through the leisure that technology would make possible. However, he had subsequently come to see that technology is not simply an indifferent means that can be applied to whatever end we choose. Technology shapes our ends, and, finally, becomes our end. Therefore, it is foolish to think that we can first pursue mastery of the world and then devote ourselves to truth after we have achieved it, because in the pursuit of mastery, truth is destroyed. Truth as defined by Simone Weil, one of Grant's great teachers, is "the radiant manifestation of reality."[22] It is evident as beauty, and it is known through love of what is. But in the drive to master nature, this radiance is extinguished. The order of things is riven in two: love and the apprehension of beauty become subjective states with no foundation in nature, while reliable knowledge comes to depend on our holding the world apart from us as an object. What he had failed to recognize, Grant said, was "the dominance of technique over all aspects of our lives."[23] In supposing that technical progress and an absolute morality might be capable of reconciliation, he had overlooked the fact that "technique is our morality" (iv).

What had changed Grant's mind, at a theoretical level, was his encounter with the writings of the German-American political philosopher Leo Strauss, then at the University of Chicago. In outlining his predicament at the end of *Philosophy in the Mass Age* Grant had said that such a predicament could only be addressed by someone who was immersed in the history of philosophy. Strauss fit this description exactly, and Grant in his introduction to the 1966 edition of

Philosophy in the Mass Age said that he counted his recent acquaintance with Strauss's thought "a high blessing"(ix). Rather than specializing in either ancient or modern thought, Strauss had thought about them together, exactly as Grant was trying to do. He convinced Grant that there was a fundamental incompatibility between ancient and modern accounts of politics, which made any reconciliation between them unthinkable. For Strauss, moreover, the ancient account was clearly superior to the bad bargain on which he thought that modernity was based:

> Oblivion of eternity, or, in other words, es-
> trangement from man's deepest desire, and
> therewith from the primary issues, is the
> price which modern man had to pay, from
> the very beginning, for attempting to be
> absolutely sovereign, to become the master
> and owner of nature, to conquer chance.[24]

Strauss began his account of modernity with the writings of Niccolò Machiavelli (1469–1527). Machiavelli, according to Strauss, argued that "one must lower the standards [of political probity] in order to make probable, if not certain, the actualization of the right or desirable social order, or in order to conquer chance . . . one must effect a shift of emphasis from moral character to institutions"(46). Ancient political philosophy as typified by Plato had seen human beings as longing, however obscurely, for the good. Machiavelli saw the passions as fundamental and regarded himself as the prophet of a new order which could achieve more humane results on less humane premises. He believed that justice was always based on injustice because societies are generally founded on revolutionary crimes. Virtue, in his account, was conventional, rather than being the result of some innate disposition. Therefore, unrealistic demands on moral character should be replaced by institutions capable of channelling the passions to moral ends.

Premodern philosophers saw virtue as the end of political life and defined the best regime as an order likely to produce such excellence. Machiavelli viewed civic virtue as a political means, a convenient fiction subject to manipulation in the interests of some greater common good. In the hope of founding politics on a surer footing than the uncertain chance of moral excellence, he instituted the characteristic modern divorce between means and ends. As Strauss explains,

> The classics thought that, owing to the weakness, or dependence of human nature, universal happiness is impossible, and therefore, they did not dream of a fulfillment of History and hence not a meaning of History . . . Because they saw how limited man's power is they held that the actualization of the best regime depends on chance. Modern man, dissatisfied with utopias and scorning them, has tried to find a guarantee for the actualization of the best social order. In order to succeed . . . he had to lower the goal of man. One form in which this was done was to replace moral virtue by universal recognition, or to replace happiness by the satisfaction deriving from universal recognition. The classical solution is

utopian in the sense that its actualization is improbable. The modern solution is utopian in the sense that its actualization is impossible. The classical solution supplies a stable standard by which to judge of any actual order. The modern solution eventually destroys the very idea of a standard that is independent of actual situations. (131)

Modernity, according to Strauss, had unfolded in what he called three waves. The first wave comprised thinkers like Thomas Hobbes and John Locke who made "the murderous Machiavell," as Shakespeare had still called him, respectable in England. They differed from Machiavelli on the character of the passions animating political life, substituting self-preservation (Hobbes) and the acquisition of property (Locke) in the place that Machiavelli had given to glory; but they agreed in founding politics on an account of human nature much reduced from what ancient philosophy had claimed for it. The second wave of modernity involved the discovery of history. Hobbes and Locke had argued that humans were made social only by entering into a self-interested contract with their fellows, but neither had doubted that there is such a thing as human nature or that it possesses aboriginally the rationality that a society based on contract implies. Second wave thinkers like Jean-Jacques Rousseau and Hegel asserted that rational human nature is not a given but develops historically. However, they still believed that history has a purpose and an inner direction. Only with the third contemporary wave of modernity, initiated before its time in the nineteenth century by Nietzsche, was this fundamental confidence shaken. Nietzsche agreed with the thinkers of the second wave that history is a horizon beyond which we cannot see, but he denied that it has any inherent meaning.

Strauss put forward these ideas in a book published in the same year as *Philosophy in the Mass Age*. It was called *What Is Political Philosophy?* and it also included a rejoinder to Alexandre Kojève, a French scholar who had written a commentary on Strauss's earlier book *On Tyranny: An Interpretation of Xenophon's Hiero*. Kojève had lectured on Hegel in Paris between 1933 and 1939, and these lectures, published as *Introduction to the Reading of Hegel*, had been so influential that Hugh Gillis believes "it is not too much to say that the subsequent history of French philosophy involves a thinking with and against Alexandre Kojève's interpretation of Hegel."[25] Grant believed that the dispute between Strauss and Kojève was "the most important controversy in contemporary political philosophy," and in 1964 he added a commentary of his own to the discussion.[26]

The Strauss-Kojève debate turned on precisely the point that Grant had left up in the air in *Philosophy in the Mass Age*: whether history moves towards some final fulfillment and whether such an "end of history"[27] is to be desired. The end towards which history is moving, according to Kojève, is "the universal and homogeneous state." (The exact words are Grant's paraphrase of Kojève.) "'Universal,'" Grant says, "implies a worldwide state, which eliminates the curse of war among nations; homogeneous means that all men would be equal, and war among classes would be eliminated."[28]

Progress towards such an order, Grant continues, is "the dominant ethical 'ideal' to which our contemporary society appeals for meaning in its activity."[29] Kojève believed it to be the only completely just order because he thought that only in a regime founded on universal equality and universal recognition would each individual be able to actualize his or her potentialities.

Strauss rejected Kojève's argument a priori because he did not believe that the truth sought by philosophers could be realized in time. Philosophy in his view sought intimations of a timeless order. But he also argued that Kojève's final regime, should it be realized, would destroy the very possibility of human excellence. A universal state, Strauss said, would require the liberation of technology from all restraint. This would eventually destroy the conditions through which excellence, or virtue, is able to manifest itself. Work, war, and class conflict have been scourges of human hope, but they have also been the forges in which the virtues were tempered. To aspire to end or overcome "the human condition" by technological means is to destroy the conditions necessary to wisdom, heroism, and productive work.

Strauss also claimed that the universal and homogeneous state would ultimately destroy philosophy. The practice of philosophy, he thought, makes manifest a natural inequality in people's disposition to think, and the universal state would have to deny or suppress any inequality. Kojève followed Hegel in believing that at the end of history philosophy would be a path open to all. Strauss believed that only a few would ever seek wisdom. And since he regarded contemplation as higher than "universal recognition," the good promised in the final state, he argued that the free and equal worldwide state would actually be a frightful tyranny.

At the time he wrote *Philosophy in the Mass Age* Grant's mind was finely poised between his Christian commitment to an absolute morality and the promise of "a new age of reason," hinted at in the "high self-consciousness" and "immense . . . open[ness] to both good and evil"[30] that he had found among his students at Dalhousie in the 1950s. Strauss tipped the balance by making what Grant regarded as a decisive argument at a crucial moment. But for this very reason, it's easy to exaggerate Strauss's "influence." Grant had a quite sincere sense, I think, of his own intellectual limitations. On a number of occasions he spoke of his dependence on "the great thinkers and the saints,"[31] for guidance. In this case, he respected the breadth and depth of Strauss's reading in political philosophy and the wisdom of his judgements. But in no sense, did he ever become a follower or an uncritical admirer of Strauss. He differed from Strauss, for example, on the part the United States was then playing in the world. Strauss and his acolytes saw the United States as a conservative guardian of Western tradition, while for Grant the U.S. was the furthest thing from a conservative society; it was "a dynamic empire spearheading the age of progress"[32] and therefore the main agent of homogenization throughout the world. Grant also differed from Strauss on the question of whether the cultivation of philosophy is humanity's highest end. Strauss, in Grant's view, tended to identify virtue too exclusively with understanding, and not enough with charity.[33] "It is not by philosophy that it has pleased

God to save his people," Saint Ambrose of Milan had said in the fourth century of the Christian era; and even as he wrestled with this idea, Grant knew that for him as a Christian it was finally true.

In his rejection of the religion of progress, and in his growing sense that technology had become the autonomous, self-validating core of Western civilization, Grant had taken a decisive turn. He increasingly came to believe that Western civilization was in the grip of a destiny so deeply woven into the pattern of its institutions that contemporary people confronted it not as a choice but as "the tight circle of the modern fate." "The decisions of western men over many centuries," he wrote in 1967, "have made our world too ineluctably what it is for there to be any facile exit."[34] But he did not for this reason retreat from politics or social concern. Even in the essay on the Strauss-Kojève debate, in which he opted for ancient as opposed to modern philosophy, he still acknowledged that "no writing about technological progress and the rightness of imposing limits upon it should avoid expressing the fact that the poor, the diseased, the hungry and the tired can hardly be expected to contemplate any such limitation with the equanimity of the philosopher" (103). When the Cooperative Commonwealth Federation rechristened itself the New Democratic Party in 1961, Grant contributed an essay celebrating community to the book that was published to honour this event. "The community," he wrote, "has an obligation to ease by compensation the insecurity of those sacrificed to economic progress."[35] And though he declined to stand as an NDP candidate in the federal election the following year, he worked hard for the party in his home riding of Hamilton West.

Grant's relationship with the NDP ended unhappily in 1963 when the New Democrats sided with the Liberals against Diefenbaker, an event over which Grant's anger still echoes in this interview. But the publication of *Lament for a Nation* in 1965 cemented Grant's reputation as a different kind of conservative nonetheless. In that book Grant claimed that a strong state and a strong set of public institutions, both commercial and cultural, had been essential to the preservation of Canada. Doctrinaire attachment to the liberal principles of a free market and the unrestricted play of individual interests, he said, had always threatened Canadian independence and had finally proved fatal to it during the hegemony of the Liberal Party in the twentieth century. In the face of overwhelming American influence "nationalism [in Canada] had to go hand in hand with some measure of socialism."[36] The same idea was later expressed in the popular figure of the Red Tory.[37]

Grant was certainly one of the prototypes of this figure, but what he actually said in the final sections of *Lament for a Nation* was that such a position was becoming increasingly untenable. The passages in his text that seemed to nourish the idea of the Red Tory were mostly sentences about what might have been. Grant's more disturbing contemporary import was his claim that a conservatism of the common good was no longer politically feasible. "Those who adopt that title [of conservative]," he wrote, "can be no more than the defenders of whatever structure of power is at any moment necessary to technological change" (67). When he introduced a re-issue of his text in 1970, he even questioned the extent to which Canada had ever had a truly conservative political culture. His lament, he said, had been written "too much from anger and too little from irony" (x). "The sense of a common good standing against capitalist individualism depended in English-speaking Canada on a tradition of British conservatism which was itself largely beaten in Great Britain by the time it was inherited by Canadians. Our pioneering conditions . . . made individualist capitalist greed the overwhelming force among our elite" (x). He now said that his book was not "what many people took it to be . . . a lament for the passing of a British dream of Canada. It was rather a lament for the romanticism of the original dream. Only a fool could have lived in Toronto in the 1920s and 1930s without recognizing that any British tradition of the common good which transcended contract was only a veneer" (xi).

The introduction to the second edition of *Lament for a Nation* vitiated an already thin claim, and tended to confirm the sense of some readers that his lament was really only nostalgia for the folkways of his dying social class.[38] But the way in which Grant's argument receded from any present, or even historical, possibility into a broad civilizational critique probably only increased its cachet amongst the younger generation of intellectuals. Among the radicals of the 1960s there were intimations of a new age in which old ideologies would have to be radically rethought, and this created a mood congenial to Grant's deep interrogation of modern certainties. Not long after his break with the NDP he was taken up by the New Left. There was common ground on the question of the Vietnam War, which Grant had denounced unequivocally as genocide, and on the character of the contemporary university, which Grant claimed had become a soulless techno-logical "multiversity." He was also an intense and gifted teacher, unusually open to dialogue with his students. During the 1950s in Halifax, according to Louis Greenspan, the home Grant shared with his wife, Sheila, and eventually six children was "a kind of salon for philosophy students."[39] Novelist Matt Cohen says that when he met Grant during the 1960s

> [I] was very impressed by his willingness or even eagerness to take what I said seriously . . . His whole method of teaching and of discourse was not to say what was right and what was wrong, although he certainly had his own thoughts on these questions, but it was much more of . . . a Greek approach to things, where he believed that people should lead them-selves . . . because he believed that what was right and wrong was within people, within every person . . . To him the business of living and the business of philosophy were the same thing.[40]

Grant, for his part, loved the clear thinking of the radical young about American liberalism and Ameri-can imperialism, and in 1966 he entered into conver-sation with the leaders of the Student Union for Peace Action (SUPA), the main organization of the New Left in Canada at that time. His friendships with a number of the individuals involved were long-lived, but the formal relationship soon foundered when Grant refused to participate in an illegal protest in the federal

Parliament. Nor did he ever really share the hopes of the New Left. In fact he warned against "easy hopes" when he addressed the International Teach-in in Toronto in October of 1965. Those who believe that "marching and sitting" will overcome "the emptiness and dehumanisation that this society produces," he said, are:

> indulging in . . . dangerous dreams. . . Hope in the future has been and is the chief opiate of modern life . . . Its danger is that it prevents men from looking clearly at their situation. If people have vast expectations about a society such as ours they are going to be disappointed, and then their moral fervour can turn rancid and bitter. Moral fervour is too precious a commodity not to be put into the service of reality.[41]

Grant affirmed "the nobility of protest" and applauded the efforts of the younger generation "to give meaning to citizenship in a society which by its enormity and impersonality cuts people off from the public world." He acknowledged that "the students who care enough about the world to protest are much finer than those who are interested in public affairs simply because they want to climb within the system . . . [or] those who crawl through the university simply as a guarantee of the slow road to death in the suburbs." In fact, Grant insisted to the end of his career that what was wrong with universities was not the students but the lack of moral and intellectual nourishment in the curriculum. When Robert Bothwell and David Bercuson published a book in 1984 which

Grant felt placed undue emphasis on the role of student movements in turning the university into an intellectual cafeteria, Grant responded that the students were "darlings," and their teachers ought to look more critically at their own part in what had gone wrong.[42] In his own writings he blamed professors for using research as "an excuse for avoiding the ardours of teaching,"[43] and claimed that "the best of their students think they are going to get something living from the humanities and when they find they are not opt for the real culture which is all around them."[44]

Grant admired the students he taught and knew, and he insisted, against some of the more glib analyses later made of the 1960s, that their alienation was an expression of the crisis of Western civilization and not its cause. But that ultimately was as far as he could walk with "the movement." In an essay published in *Canadian Dimension* in 1967 he said that he thought of "the source of revolutionary fervour as arising finally from a further extension of the very modernity which has brought us where we are." And he warned that "the drive for radical change in this society tends only to harden the very directions the society is already taking."[45]

This vision of "a tightening circle" in which every hope betrays us and every attempt to wriggle free only tightens our bonds was fully manifest in a collection of essays from the 1960s published under the title *Technology and Empire*. At the heart of this collection was the idea that technology is the very essence of modern persons, or as Grant says that "technique is ourselves" (137). This idea arose in Grant primarily out of his amazement at seeing the world in which he had grown up physically and spiritually transformed within a generation. It was reinforced by the fury of the aerial bombardment of Vietnam. And it was also influenced by his reading of the German philosopher Martin Heidegger, to whom Grant acknowledged a special debt on the subject of technology.

From the beginning of his career Grant had immersed himself in Continental thought in a way that was unusual for a contemporary English-speaking philosopher. Throughout the 1950s he tested his faith in the purgatorial fires of existentialism. "Sartre's play, *The Flies*," he told listeners to a commentary for CBC Radio's *Architects of Modern Thought* series in 1955, "made me understand as no other writing I have ever read what it was to see life as meaningless, to doubt the existence of God. It is so powerful that it permeated all my dreams throughout one winter."[46] Grant was later embarrassed by the fulsomeness of his praise for Sartre's artistry, and this embarrassment probably coloured his contemptuous and rather unfair remark in this interview that Sartre was "just a plagiarist of Heidegger"; but there is no doubt that he did eventually come to think of Heidegger as "the consummate thinker of our age."

As with Strauss, I think that Grant's relationship with Heidegger ought to be understood in terms of the insight Heidegger offered on a particular point rather than as influence in general. The point, again, was a crucial one, but Grant was otherwise quite ambivalent about Heidegger. (At the time I visited him he had a small photograph of Heidegger on the mantelpiece, and I noticed one morning that it was facing the wall rather than the room, as it had been the previous day.

When I asked him about this, he said that he changed the orientation depending on how he was disposed to "the old bastard" that day.) What Grant derived from his study of Heidegger was the idea that technology is something more than just the ensemble of techniques with which we can accomplish our ends. Technology, for Heidegger, is not just a manifestation of knowledge, an application of science. It is an orientation to the world, a bearing towards other beings which annihilates "things as things" and turns nature into a "stock" or "standing reserve" in which everything is available and can potentially be manipulated. Heidegger's subtle probings of this attitude helped Grant to see that within technology, knowing and making have become identical, so that all knowledge now stands under the obligation of social service, and whatever can be made ought to be made.

North America, Grant argued, had been particularly open to this sense of technology because of the way in which our heritage had combined Calvinism with frontier conditions in which effective technique was a condition of survival. "Calvin's doctrine of the Hidden God by whose inscrutable Will men were elected to salvation or damnation meant that they believed themselves cut off from the contemplation of God, except as he revealed himself in the Bible."[47] The divine could neither be represented in ritual nor discerned in nature, and "the absence of natural theology and liturgical comforts left the lonely soul face to face with the transcendent (and therefore elusive) will of God." Echoing Max Weber's analysis in *The Protestant Ethic and the Spirit of Capitalism*, Grant suggested the result was that "This will had to be sought and served not through our contemplations but directly through our practice. From the solitude and uncertainty of that position came the responsibility that could find no rest." [48]

The encounter of this "restless righteousness" with an alien land, in Grant's view, produced in North America a particularly intense and uncritical "drive to an unlimited technological future . . . in which technical reason has become so universal that it has closed down on openness and awe, questioning and listening"(24). By the later 1960s he was rendering this condition in fairly apocalyptic terms. The society that a decade before had promised a new age of reason had now taken on a sordid, desperate, nearly hallucinated quality for him. Vietnam presented "a Gorgon's face" and showed the English-speaking world at "its basest point" (11). The motto of the American Empire, he said sardonically, was "napalm abroad, the orgasm at home" (126). He found people living "in a monistic vulgarity in which nobility and wisdom have been exchanged for a pale belief in progress, alternating with boredom and weariness of spirit" (24). "A plush patina of hectic subjectivity" disguised "the iron maiden of an objectified world inhabited by increasingly objectified beings" (142). "The incredibly difficult question," he said at the end of his long meditation on "Canadian Fate and Imperialism" is "What is worth doing in the midst of this barren twilight?" (78).

Grant concluded *Technology and Empire* with what he called "A Platitude," a meditation on the fact that "All definitions of technique which place it outside ourselves hide from us what it is" (137). We incarnate technique in "our vision of ourselves as creative freedom, making ourselves and conquering the chances of an indifferent world" (137). But, if we are technology, he asks poignantly, how can we know what we have lost, or even that we have lost anything? If "freedom is the highest term in the modern language" (138), then doesn't that mean that there are no longer any purposes outside freedom by which we could determine what freedom is for? This for Grant is "the terrifying darkness"[49] that has fallen on his world: in the making of technological society we have lost the measure of what we have made. Under these circumstances, he says, we can only try to "sense our dispossession" by listening for "intimations of deprival."[50] The posture of desiring attention that Grant recommends is in some way reminiscent of Heidegger who says that in order to find our way again into "the Nearness of Being," we must "first learn to exist in the nameless."[51] But in the end, Grant seems to me much closer to Christian mysticism. There is much in common, for example, between Grant's "Platitude" and T. S. Eliot's version of the "Dark Night of the Soul" in his *Four Quartets*:

> I said to my soul, be still, and wait without hope
> For hope would be hope for the wrong thing;
>   wait without love
> For love would be love of the wrong thing;
>   there is yet faith
> But the faith and the love and the hope are all
>   in the waiting.[52]

Heidegger listened for the stirrings of new gods; Grant sought a re-collection of "what was in the beginning, is now, and ever more shall be."[53]

George Grant said in a number of places that he did

not feel himself to be at all adequate to the thorough rethinking that his conclusions about the "madness in the modern"[54] seemed to demand. His work in a sense was a prologue to this rethinking, an attempt to reveal what was missing beneath "the plush patina hectic subjectivity," and to specify the conditions under which such a rethinking might become possible. The first step to this end was "to bring the darkness into light as darkness,"[55] to try to make as plain as possible what it was that had occurred in the civilization of Western Europe and its colonial offspring. Grant treated ideas, as his colleague Louis Greenspan has said, as "primordial historical actors,"[56] and he believed accordingly that one could discover what might be called the genetic code of an age in its greatest thinkers. His writing often involved a patient effort to tease out and elaborate the implications of this code, but only in one book did he devote himself to the explication of a single philosopher. The opportunity came as a result of an invitation from CBC Radio to do the 1969 Massey Lectures. Grant decided to devote a substantial portion of the five hours to a close reading of Nietzsche. The text was published in 1971 as *Time as History*.

In his lectures Grant explored the modern genesis of the idea of history. This idea arose, he said, as a response to the overcoming of the Aristotelian notion of purpose or final cause. In this older account a thing's cause was at the same time its "good," or what it was fitted for. The Cartesian cut between mind and nature eliminated the idea that beings had any ultimate purpose. "History" was the realm in which human purposes reappeared as willed meanings. In ancient and medieval thought, what was good was known by intuitions reaching outside time. Morality was "a desiring attention to perfection."[57] In modern thought the good was made manifest in time, and morality was "self-legislation, the willing of our values" (48).

It was in Nietzsche's writings, Grant thought, that the meaning of this shift from eternal being to eternal becoming was unveiled. Nietzsche "express[ed] modernity in its fullest." He was the first to see in Platonism and Christianity a fearful failure of nerve before the abyss of endless becoming; the first to uncover beneath every moral imposture a tortured "will to power"; the first to make the quintessentially modern statement that "art is worth more than truth";[58] and the first to embrace the fate that had made men "masters of the earth" in the hope that this "love of fate [would] guarantee that dynamic willing shall be carried on by lovers of the earth and not by those twisted by hatred and hysteria against existing."[59] In exploring Nietzsche's thought, Grant hoped to bring to light the darkness that he thought was latent in the tangled and unphilosophical thoughts of his contemporaries. He was struck, for example, by the unthinking ease with which clergy and other moralists used the term "values." This term, according to Grant, is the epitome of Nietzsche's thought. It implies that what we call good is nothing more than an arbitrary existential choice, without any foundation in nature and enforceable against other "values" only by the resoluteness of our choice. A common phrase like "religious values" is, therefore, an oxymoron, a comforting illusion that conflates a realm in which truth is founded on reason with a realm in which truth's only foundation is in the will. Speaking about values evokes morality while simultaneously denying that morality has any substance. A close public reading of Nietzsche, Grant thought, was a way of bringing such contradictions into the light and challenging the divided mind that allows us to keep speaking of right and wrong even as we recognize that we are actually "beyond good and evil."

Grant continued "bringing the darkness into light as darkness" in a second set of lectures delivered at Mount Allison University in 1974, and published as *English-Speaking Justice*. Justice had always had a central place in Grant's thinking; but here, for the first time, he reflected at length on the liberal theory of justice as a contractual relation between self-interested parties. Grant claimed that the moral vacuity of this liberal theory had been obscured by its close relationship with Protestant Christianity. Liberalism and Protestantism had, in effect, been born together, and this sibling relationship had generated the illusion that the moral vigour of Protestantism somehow belonged to liberalism as well. This happened particularly among English-speaking peoples because they were so much less philosophical than Germans, and this left them "enfolded more than they knew in long memories and hopes."[60] Only when Protestantism began to fade as an authentic moral force, and judges and legislators had to rely on the liberal theory of justice alone, did the moral weakness of that theory become evident.

Grant found the paradigm of this denuded theory in the reasoning of Mr. Justice Blackmun of the American Supreme Court in Roe v. Wade. This was the 1973 case in which the court ruled "that no state has the right to pass legislation which would prevent a citizen from receiving an abortion during the first six months of pregnancy."[61] "The decision," Grant said, revealed "modern liberalism in its pure contractual form: right prior to good; a foundational contract protecting individual rights; the neutrality of the state concerning moral 'values'; [and] social pluralism supported by and supporting this neutrality." But though this decision might appear "liberal" in its defence of individuals against the power of "moral majorities," he went on, it actually "raise[d] a cup of poison to the lips of liberalism" (75). In denying consideration to the fetus, Grant said, the court was making "an ontological distinction between members of the same species." In making such a distinction it was inevitably faced with the question of what a human being is. But this was precisely the question liberalism couldn't answer because of the doctrine that right is prior to good; i.e. that contentious questions about what is good — in this case what is good about human beings — must be left to the conscience of the individual while the state concerns itself only with the delineation and enforcement of rights. As a result, according to Grant, the court dealt arbitrarily with the question it could not answer by denying the fetus the status of person.

Grant had always made it clear to his admirers on the left that he was a conservative, but what he meant by this term was easily overlooked when questions were discussed abstractly, as they often were in such books as *Time as History* and *Technology and Empire*. *English-Speaking Justice* brought a parting of the ways. Access to abortion was a key plank in the platform of official feminism, and feminism, after the 1960s was the heart of "progressive" thinking. Grant's opposition was unequivocal. He argued vigorously in popular media against "the mass killing of the weakest members of our species."[62] This brought him into a political alliance on the right where he fitted even more uneasily than he had on the left. He sometimes found it extremely hard, as he said in this interview, to find himself allied with people whose views he considered "atrocious" on other questions, such as nuclear weapons, but the way he understood the abortion question left him no choice.

To Grant, abortion on demand represented a further step in the subjugation of the spontaneity of nature, "a triumph of the will"[63] over the chance of existence, a final domestication of the power, and sacredness, of sex in the interests of self-determination and self-control. And it came, he thought, at a terrible cost: judicially sanctioned murder of the innocent. The question had been framed by those favouring unrestricted access to abortion in terms of women's rights. But to Grant there was a conflict of rights, since to his mind the fetus was also a being to whom consideration was due. When Mr. Justice Blackmun allowed the stronger and more articulate of these rights to completely extinguish the weaker claim, he revealed the crucial moral flaw in liberalism. A contractual theory of justice, according to Grant, does not assert that there is something about human beings that makes them inherently worthy of rights, it holds only that they have vested rights in each other by virtue of a founding contract made in their mutual interest. This did not matter so long as people believed a Christianity that upheld the ultimate worth of human personality; but when Christianity lost its central place, the weakness of the idea of justice as nothing more than selfishness enlightened by fear was revealed. This, to Grant, was "the terrifying darkness which [had] fallen on modern justice."[64] A fetus, in his view, was an ensouled being equal before God with all other human beings, but the institutions of liberal justice no longer knew of any reason why it should not be killed if its existence was inconvenient. Grant found this frightening in itself, and frightening also in the precedent he thought it set. More open acceptance of euthanasia and the development of criteria by which to measure the "quality of life" among the aged and among newborns with disabilities seemed to him to point in a similar direction. As Western societies more openly asked, with Nietzsche's lunatic prophet Zarathustra, "Who shall be the lord of the earth?"[65] might not other citizens too weak to enforce their claims also find themselves undeserving of justice?

Much of George Grant's writing followed what was called in theology the *via negativa*, the attempt to reveal what is good not by a positive statement but by the clearing away of obstacles and impostures. Only in his last book, *Technology and Justice*, in an essay called "Faith and the Multiversity," did he attempt any sustained statement about "the truth of what is not present in the modern." The essay was a long meditation about "the dependence of what we know on what we love" (72). In it he revealed for the first time the outlines of the reading of Plato and the Gospels implicit in so much of his earlier work, but never spelled out.

"Faith and the Multiversity" also hinted at the importance of the thought of Simone Weil for Grant. Simone Weil was born to a family of secular Jews in Paris in 1909, and converted to Christianity in the later 1930s. She died in England in 1943, while working for the French provisional government. Most of her writings were published posthumously. The first collection of her essays and letters to appear in English came out in 1951 under the title *Waiting for God*. The CBC asked Grant to review it, and he continued to read her work thereafter. In 1958, after a long wrestle with her thought during a train journey to Edmonton, he wrote to his wife that, even though he found her "absolute mysticism . . . tiring," he was convinced that she was "nearer the truth than anyone else."[66] By the mid-1960s, after visiting Weil's mother and her friend and biographer, Simone Pétrement, he had concluded that Simone Weil was a modern saint. The saints, to Grant, were those who had "given themselves away" and become, at the cost of everything, transparent to the truth. Simone Weil's sanctity gave her a dimension that was absent in those people, like Leo Strauss, to whose thinking Grant felt indebted. He approached her life and work more tentatively and with greater awe, declining to write about her, even as he came to feel an absolute confidence in the purity and consistency of her thought. "Beside Strauss," Grant once said, "Simone Weil is a flame."[67]

What Weil offered Grant was a way of thinking about Christianity that avoided the two great pitfalls into which Grant thought Western civilization had fallen: the split between religion and science, which left the minds of thinking people divided between apparently antagonistic cosmologies; and the notion of time as history, with its consequent "oblivion of eternity." Weil believed that Western Christianity had succumbed very early in its history to a blasphemous conception of the divine which set aside the proto-Christian genius of Greece in favour of the worst

elements of the Jewish and Roman civilizations. In the
Gospels, she said, as in the sacred texts of China,
India, and Greece, providence was represented as the
unvarying order of things. "Heaven's net is vast, its
meshes are wide," Lao Tzu had said, "but nothing
gets through."[68] Jesus continually compared the
Kingdom of Heaven to the operations of Nature. He
asked his followers to "consider the lilies of the field,"
and evoked the Kingdom of God by analogy with "the
earth [which] brings forth fruit of herself."[69] When he
taught his disciples to be perfect "even as your Father
which is in heaven is perfect," his image of God's perfection was that he "makes his sun to rise on the evil
and the good, and sends rain on the just and the
unjust."[70] God was portrayed not as a personal being
toying capriciously with his people, but as an impar-
tial, unvarying, and trusted order. This changed, Weil
thought, "when the Christian religion was officially
adopted by the Roman Empire." Drawing on those
elements in the Old Testament that portrayed
"Jehovah's juridical relationship to the Hebrews [as]
that of a master to his slaves . . . God was turned into
a counterpart of the Emperor."[71]

Weil believed that this displacement of an impersonal by a personal notion of providence had had
fateful consequences for the West. In *The Republic*
Plato distinguished between the order of necessity
and the order of good, and said that a great distance
separated these orders. This distance is reflected in
what Weil called "the non-intervention of God in the
operation of grace."[72] "Everything that has happened,"
she says, "whatever it may be, is in accordance with
the will of the almighty Father."[73] The very mystery of

Christ's passion is that God does not intervene in it, that "God can only be present in creation under the form of absence."[74] Providence, as we experience it, is identical with necessity or chance. The good transcends us. What happened in Western Christianity, according to both Grant and Weil, was that this "ambiguous mystery"[75] was set aside by a triumphalist church that claimed it embodied the will of God and that it could, through its sacraments, constrain and certify this will. "Western Christianity," in Grant's terms, "simplified the divine love by identifying it too closely with immanent power in the world." By recklessly setting aside the "agnostic affirmations" originally present in Plato and the Gospels, and claiming that "providence is scrutable," the Western church tended to succumb to "the great lie that evil is good and good evil."[76]

Grant also followed Simone Weil in recognizing that it was this corruption of Christianity that had eventually generated "the absolute incompatibility between the spirit of religion, and that of science, . . . [which] leaves the soul in a state of secret, unacknowledged uneasiness."[77] For Weil there was nothing unscientific about religion — she found in the Gospels "a supernatural physics of the human soul" (265) and believed that "The entire works of St. John of the Cross are nothing else but a strictly scientific study of supernatural mechanisms" (264). Nor was there anything irreligious about the study of nature — "The savant's true aim," she said, "is the union of his own mind with the mysterious wisdom eternally inscribed in the universe . . . Scientific investigation is simply a form of religious contemplation" (262). The trouble was that by embodying God in history and making historical progress in overcoming necessity the image of God's will, Western Christianity had disembedded the divine from Nature and destroyed the analogy between necessity and the Kingdom of God. As a result, and despite the devout character of many early modern scientists, science conceived itself as the exploration of a world without final purpose in which love granted no insight and beauty made no allusion to truth. When Nietzsche finally proclaimed that "Truth is ugly"[78] he brought into the open what had been implied in modern science from the beginning.

The triumphalist theology that developed in Roman Christianity was also connected, in Grant's view, to the fateful emphasis on the will which expressed itself in the restless technological dynamism of Western civilization. "The idea of creation," to Grant was "an abyss in which our minds are swallowed up." But Western Christians, he said, had come to think of it as "an act of [divine] self-expansion."[79] "Willing was exalted through the stamping proclamations of the creating Will."[80] This strenuous, expansive conception of divinity led to an account of religion as the exercise of will, rather than as the pursuit of knowledge. From its origins, Grant thought, the West had inherited two incompatible accounts of will. From the ancient Greeks had come a tradition that "freedom was the gift of truth, which we acquired through our reason," while from the Jewish scriptures had come a view that freedom was something "primal," "something that human beings had absolutely as human beings."[81] This second account was related to a conception of divinity as personal will, rather than impersonal law. Grant believed it had fed the emphasis on the mastery of nature in technological society.

Simone Weil helped Grant to understand creation in a very different way. For her, Grant wrote, "creation is a withdrawal, an act of love, involved with all the suffering and renunciation and willing to let the other be, that are given in the idea of love."[82] God is present to us as a loving consent to our existence that can only be expressed as absence. "He is our Father, who is in heaven," she wrote in her commentary on the Lord's Prayer. "If we think to have a Father here below it is not he, it is a false God. We cannot take a single step towards him. We do not walk vertically. We can only turn our eyes toward him. We do not have to search for him, we only have to change the direction in which we are looking. It is for him to search for us."[83]

Simone Weil never became a member of the Roman Catholic Church because, as she wrote to the priest who longed to baptize her, "The love of those things that are outside visible Christianity keeps me outside the Church."[84] In this respect, as well, she furthered both Grant's thinking and his work in building the Department of Religion at McMaster University between 1961 and 1980, by demonstrating an approach to Christianity that was intellectually honest, non-dogmatic, and open to other ways of understanding the divine. She believed that the same truth that was manifest in Christianity had been manifest in all the ancient civilizations. "The children of God," she said, "should not have any other country here below but the universe itself, with the totality of all the reasoning creatures it ever has contained, contains, or ever will contain . . . Christ has bidden us to attain to the perfection of our heavenly Father by imitating his indiscriminate bestowal of light. Our intelligence too should have the same complete impartiality."[85]

Weil allowed Grant to distinguish between Christianity as such and the triumphalist, post-Augustinian Christianity which he thought had produced our modern technomania. Believing that "it is not wise to criticize Christianity in public these days, when so many journalists and intellectuals prove their status by such criticism,"[86] Grant said relatively little about this matter, but in this interview and in "Faith and the Multiversity," which he was working on at the time he spoke to me, he said quite clearly that he thought Christianity needed to be "reformulated." This reformulation would involve relearning "the truth about the distance which separates the orders of good and necessity." Only on this basis, he thought, could beauty and truth be reconciled and people released from the modern prison house of groundless subjectivity.

"Faith and the Multiversity" quite decisively refutes the charge of pessimism that was so often laid against Grant, a charge which irked him by seeming to deny his faith. The essay shows him as quite willing to believe that in time "the modern mistake" can be unmade. In this sense he was a lot more hopeful than his many contemporaries who had resigned themselves to life without "intimations of perfection." He was seen as pessimist, I think, mainly because he insisted so adamantly on the enclosed and self-perpetuating qualities of an existence in which technology has become the horizon of moral concern. Once he had understood that "oblivion of eternity" was not just a philosophical deception but something in the marrow of a society determined to master chance and become its own providence, he could not avoid wondering whether this might be a terminal condition, in which people would no longer have any way of "knowing that they didn't know," and every attempt at "radical" reform would only repeat the original mistake. And so, like T. S. Eliot in "Ash Wednesday," he could only pray, "Teach us to sit still." How, in what he believed was so tight a bind, could he counsel more than a purgatorial effort to abstain from sentimental illusions and listen for what we have lost?

Grant thought that nearly all modern persons were living in a grotesque philosophical confusion. This resulted, in the first place, from the sheer difficulty of thinking through the situation into which we have been, as Heidegger says, "thrown," but it was also a consequence of our belonging to a long tradition which had inherited from its several origins incompatible ideas about things, and which was continuously encrusting these ideas with new inconsistencies. Most of the people, most of the time, he believed, are obliged to deploy words and ideas ready-made. They have all sorts of things on their minds other than philosophical consistency, often very desirable things, and therefore use what comes ready to hand. This works very well so long as what is handed over to people through their traditions is a stock of sound ideas and well-understood words. But when these traditions break down, people are at the mercy of the ill-assorted, ill-considered ideas that are pitched at them from every side. Under these circumstances, Grant thought, the public role of the philosopher is to attempt a systematic clarification. As novelist Matt Cohen has said,

Grant's method of teaching was "to make people take what they thought seriously."[87] This was also his method of writing — to try to reveal the generative thoughts that people were half-consciously thinking as they went about their everyday affairs.

Even to have attempted this task was a sign, not of pessimism, but of hope that philosophy could still be undertaken on behalf of a community and not just as a specialized profession. Grant, moreover, didn't just speak of this hope; he embodied it in a way open to emulation by others. His friend and editor Dennis Lee has said that Grant was "a witness [whose] primary vocation in writing was to suffer with all his mind, and all his body, heart and soul, the emergence of the nihilism, which had been unfolding over the past centuries within the project of modernity."[88] This gave his writing a quality of deep and vivid feeling which enlivened an otherwise highly abstract style. It doesn't come out much in this interview because the talk was mostly of philosophy, but throughout his life Grant was a lover of music and of literature. In journal extracts quoted by his biographer William Christian he is shown again and again as immersed in the music of Mozart, the poetry of Baudelaire, or the novels of Henry James. He published essays on Dostoyevsky and the French novelist Céline.[89] He was a lover of the Canadian landscape, finding beauty in "the curves and lights of rock and sea in a North Atlantic bay,"[90] as much as in "the tenderness and exquisiteness" of Mozart's *Magic Flute*, which he thought was "like partaking of eternity."[91] And these loves imparted glints of lyricism to even the most dense of his formulations. The highest attribute of the good, for him, was that it is lovable, and it was by inspiring love that he led people to philosophy.

George Grant's work revolved around the question of whether human beings can have confident knowledge of a truth outside time and space, or whether all knowledge is finally conditioned by our circumstances. And like St. Exupéry's little prince, once he got hold of a question, he wouldn't let go of it, no matter how often he was accused of nostalgia, naïveté, or professional incompetence. In his first book, *Philosophy in the Mass Age*, he wrote that limits to human freedom can only finally consist in "a reality we must accept, not a value we create." "God," he concluded, "is that which we cannot manipulate. He is the limit of our right to change the world. In the recognition of limit, the idea of law in some form must once again become real for us."[92] When he realized that modern historicism made the revival of natural law in any form impossible, he continued to testify to his "simple incomprehension" at how anyone could be reconciled to a fate in which unlimited human self-assertion was the highest good. "I do not understand how anybody could love fate, unless within the details of our fates there could appear, however rarely, intimations of . . . perfection."[93] At the end of his life, in his last writings, he was still asking about the "deep disjunction which has fallen on our western existence — the disjunction between beauty and truth."[94]

Looking back on Grant's work today, one can certainly criticize it. From the point of view of philosopher Charles Taylor, who has written against excessively monolithic accounts of modernity and argued that we can "retrieve" certain worthwhile modern aspirations

without accepting the entire package,[95] Grant is open
to the challenge of having made his portrait of the age
too starkly black and white. From the point of view of
German historian Barbara Duden, who has tried to
argue that a fetus is not a citizen or a member of our
species but a ghostly product of the invasive visual-
ization technologies that turn women inside out and
make of their wombs a strange virtual public space,[96]
it is possible to fault Grant for not having seen the part
technological science has played in generating the abortion debate. One might also take exception to certain of
Grant's predictions. It is now evident, for example,
that whatever the destination of technological society
turns out to be, so far, it is not well described as the universal and homogeneous state. The postmodern
condition has turned out to be stranger, more various,
and more "historical," in terms of the persistence of
religion, war, and class conflict, than Grant foresaw.

Even these criticisms, however, testify to a certain
continuing strength in Grant's work. For me this
strength above all is in the way he brings the most important questions before us, and the poetical, deeply
suffered clarity with which he expresses them. Grant
was engaged in what I think is the most important
task of our time: the writing of what Ivan Illich once
called "a constitution of limits." Only within limits is
there any hope of shoring up memory and finding a
way out of the labyrinth of endless overcoming, back
to what every civilization, including our own, once
recognized as the human condition. I think the conversation that follows still sheds light on that way.

I

BEYOND TIME AND SPACE, THERE IS ORDER

DAVID CAYLEY: Your father was the headmaster at Upper Canada College. So you must have grown up living at the school?

GEORGE GRANT: Indeed, and I found it hard to go to school at a place run by my father. I felt somebody might take me as a spy. The thing about youth is that often one doesn't know quite what is happening. When something is difficult, one knows it, without understanding the real reason, and this is why youth is hard.

CAYLEY: What sort of man was your father?

GRANT: My father was a Nova Scotian, who'd grown up in Kingston, Ontario. He was essentially a very gentle, strong scholar, who I think, above all, was ruined by the First World War. I mean, he was ruined physically — he was terribly wounded. I don't mean ruined as a human being, but I think the war was terrible for people who had grown up in the great era of progress. To suddenly meet the *holocaust* of the trenches head-on like my father did — it was just terrible!

This was a prodigious experience for people of that era. You even more than I have grown up in a world where one takes it for granted that this is just the way the world is. But it was quite hard for me to leave the progressive liberalism of the nineteenth century because of the second war, and I think for these people it was even harder. The first war made a very great impression on my father.

CAYLEY: In what sort of world did your father grow up?

GRANT: Well, my grandfather lived just at that high point in Canadian life at the end of the nineteenth century when protestantism and liberalism were identified, and people could really believe in them together. He went on the first survey of the CPR across Canada. He lived in the same town and was a friend of John A. Macdonald, and they were really confident that their kind of liberal protestantism would rule the world.

I think on the whole the liberalism came first with my grandfather. You see, in that generation, to become a minister of the protestant church really meant something and many ambitious people chose the career for that reason.

CAYLEY: He was the principal of Queen's?

GRANT: Yes . . . I think part of my father's great gentleness was that he'd had a very dominating father, which led him to be much gentler with people.

CAYLEY: What were the consequences of his experiences in the war, as far as his outlook was concerned?

GRANT: Well, if you're talking of practical consequences, he gave a lot of his life to enormous support of the League of Nations, and all this kind of thing. He was much more open than his father had been. He sent money to Mr. Woodsworth, who was head of the CCF, which, from his world, wouldn't have been natural to him. The war led my father into a lot of reform, and into an optimism about reform that would have been part of his liberalism in any case, but became more intense because of the war. Of course, he didn't live so very long after the war, because he'd been badly hurt.

CAYLEY: What do you mean by his liberalism?

GRANT: Well, I mean by a liberal somebody who believes man's essence is his freedom. *Freedom* and *liberal* just mean the same thing, really. *Liberal* just means free, doesn't it? And this has been the dominating spirit of the English-speaking world. It is so deeply a part of the English-speaking world, to which Canada belongs, that people just take it for granted, in a certain sense, that man is free and is going to make the world as he wills.

CAYLEY: And when you speak of your grandfather as having been at the height of the identification of liberalism and protestantism, presumably you are implying a subsequent decline.

GRANT: Yes. Protestantism as an authentic force has gradually died. And here, I think, you can't get away from the enormous shock people got from Darwin. There had been a turning away from Christianity a century before, but this was the first mass turning away in the English-speaking world, and it happened first in England, then in the United States, and slightly later in Canada.

Protestantism in my grandfather was still a vital force. Now, I think it is true that modern liberalism, in its English-speaking form, can't do very well without some great force behind it. Liberalism, in a way, helped to destroy protestantism, but it destroyed something that had immensely supported it. You can't look at the history of the English-speaking world without seeing that the Protestants were always on the liberals' side. Other forms of Christianity, until recently, were much more against liberal doctrine. Catholicism was the great sustaining enemy of the doctrine of progress. But what I'm saying about Canadian history is that liberalism has become tired in the modern world, hasn't it? — without the sustaining force of protestantism. That's all I'm saying.

CAYLEY: What was your own formation as a Christian?

GRANT: Well there's always something extremely egocentric in talking about these matters, but I've mentioned the great, sane, secular liberalism on which I was brought up and I'm sure the second war, the violence of it, just broke that for me.

The second war to me — I'm just talking about my experience — was an unqualified disaster. This led me, to use the old-fashioned language, to be converted. I had deserted the Merchant Navy because I had found out I had tuberculosis. I went down into the country. I was young and full of passion — passion in a broad sense, not just the limited sense in which we now talk about it. I just remember going off to work one morning and I remember walking through a gate;

I got off my bicycle and walked through a gate, and I believed in God. I can't tell you more, I just knew that was it for me. And that came to me very suddenly. I don't mean that in any very dramatic sense; I just mean it as the case, because I'd come from a world where the idea of, I don't like to call it "the idea of God," but where God had not been taken terribly seriously. Religion was something that was good for a society and kept people in order, but really, if you explored it intellectually, it was B.S., it was nonsense. This was a prodigious moment for me.

CAYLEY: This experience of going through the gate and knowing — can you say what it was that you knew?

GRANT: I think it was a kind of affirmation that beyond time and space there is order. Now, all the psychologists and psychiatrists could just say that I was looking for order, but for me it was an affirmation about what is, an affirmation that ultimately there is order. And that is what one means by God, isn't it? That ultimately the world is not a maniacal chaos — I think that's what the affirmation was.

CAYLEY: Can you tell me a bit more about the war-time experiences that had led up to this?

GRANT: I was a pacifist, and the first thing I did, which was a great experience for me, was to become the air raid warden in charge of a large part of the Surrey Docks while they were being bombed by the Germans.[97] I saw a lot of people killed, I dragged people out. I saw this in detail. In a way I was ashamed of being a pacifist and wanted to show that it wasn't from fear that I rejected the war, so I was very much involved in the violence of the bombing of London; I was right at the heart of it. Then when the Russians came into the war in '41 — people should always remember this if they're attacking the Russians — it meant England wasn't bombed any more; everything now turned on this terrible destruction of the Slavs. Therefore, I knew there was going to be no more bombing. I was looking for something I could do, and I went into the Merchant Navy, and then got TB.

CAYLEY: And then you say that you deserted. I don't know how to take that.

GRANT: Well, when they found I had TB, they wouldn't take me on board a ship. I went in for a test and they found that I was no good in the lungs, so I just ran away. It wasn't exactly deserting. I just was appalled. Luckily, my uncle represented Canada in England at this time, and he found me very shortly and shipped me home very quickly. I then convalesced from the TB in Canada.[98]

CAYLEY: After you ran away, you worked on a farm?

GRANT: Yes, before my uncle found me. Representing Canada in England, he had standing with the police, and it was very easy to find me. I was living poetically. When one is young, one can live poetically.

I just was appalled by this refusal by the medical people, and I went and got a job on a farm. My uncle soon found where I was; he got me on a ship and I was put into bed and recovered in Canada.

CAYLEY: I want to dwell for a minute more on your experience of conversion. In the interview that was published in the book *George Grant in Process* you described it as knowing that ultimately you didn't belong to yourself. I found that a very compelling description because it seemed to say so much about how your thinking subsequently developed.

GRANT: This is what belief is, is it not? As people have said within belief, hell is to be one's own. Do you remember Marlowe's *Faustus*, where Faust says to Mephistopheles, "Why aren't you in hell?" And Mephistopheles just says, "Why, this is hell, nor am I out of it." Having been turned away from the face of God, I am in hell. This is what traditional Christianity has always meant, hasn't it?

Now, talking about this sounds as if one is setting oneself up, and I don't want to imply in any way that this has made me some kind of great person. Certainly, I don't live a terribly good life. It's probably made me better than I otherwise would have been, but that's not terribly good. I think it's very hard to talk about Christianity because some people think you're implying something about your own conduct, which is just nonsense.

CAYLEY: I didn't think you were saying that you became a saint, only that you touched a greater certainty than we are usually able to touch.

GRANT: There are many people in the world who think there is no such certainty to be touched. After all, what is existentialism at its core? This is why liberals in the modern world nearly all become existentialists. Existentialism at its core — its core being Nietzsche — is saying that there is no such centre to touch. And I just think there is. My thoughts have never really turned from this central thing in any way. I can now give better arguments than I could all these many years ago, but that is still the central core of what I think about.

CAYLEY: You said earlier that you had grown up

within secular liberalism. How did you learn to think about what had happened to you?

GRANT: Luckily, I was allowed to take up my scholarship at Oxford again after the war and went back and studied theology. The people at Oxford said, "You just really want to study philosophic theology." Oxford was very good, there wasn't all this B.S. that is now present in PhDs; they had very little of that. I was very lucky. I was allowed to study and I was given a thesis on an outstanding Scottish liberal theologian of the nineteenth century, a man called John Oman, utterly unknown to me at first, a fellow who'd gone to Cambridge later on. And then somebody nice here, at Dalhousie, gave me a job teaching philosophy, and I realized I didn't really know very much to teach. Luckily there was a very remarkable philosopher here who taught me, and by being taught, I could teach. I really didn't know very much, but like so many people, by teaching it I came to enter into philosophy.

CAYLEY: Who were your teachers at Oxford?

GRANT: My greatest teacher, certainly by a long way, was a man called A. D. Lindsay, who was head of the college I went to. Later, because the Labour Party had nobody in the House of Lords and Lindsay was a strong Labour man, he went into the House of Lords just to give them some representation. He had translated Plato's *Republic* and some other things, and was just a very sane, sensible Scot, who appealed to me.

CAYLEY: I believe Austin Farrer was also one of your teachers?

GRANT: Yes . . . I went to hear Farrer lecture on Descartes and I fell in love. I knew this was why I had come to Oxford. I suddenly heard a great philosopher like Descartes being wonderfully articulated and so I always went to his lectures. It was sheer love. This was what had been so deeply absent in North America: somebody who really had given his mind to the study of philosophers in the past, and who could really expound them. You know how hard it is to read people like Descartes directly, you just don't know where you are. Farrer taught me how to read; I hardly ever spoke to him, I just heard him lecture. Later on he lectured on Aristotle, and it was just wonderful for me because it gave me an entrance into how to do it. This was a highly articulate, well-educated Englishman, who was also a priest of the Anglican Church. But you know it was just wonderful for me to hear something done as well as that.

CAYLEY: What sort of things did he open you to?

GRANT: He just opened me to the philosophers he talked about. I heard philosophy being talked about very sensibly. Then at the same time there was C. S. Lewis — you know, the author of children's books and other things. He had a club called the Socratic Club, and he had people there every week who would either give the reasons against Christianity or the reasons for it, in very articulate form, and then there would be a debate afterwards. I learned an immense amount from these things. You know, Lewis was a wonderful human being, and again, enormously articulate. His writing is very simple and clear, and his speech was like that as well. He looked like a great big English butcher, who might be selling meat behind a counter, and he spoke like a butcher, just direct, clear, lucid stuff. This was a wonderful part of my education. It just helped me enormously.

CAYLEY: Who attended these meetings of the Socratic Club?

GRANT: Anybody. It was there I met my wife. There would be someone, say, who would expound why Darwinism had made Christian belief impossible; then there would be a big debate. Now, there are some people who are naturally philosophic, but I am not. I needed all this to gradually come to think about these questions. Lewis called the club after the greatest philosopher, but it was a theological as well as philosophic club, and hundreds of people went.

CAYLEY: You said that some people are natural philosophers, but that you weren't one of those. I'm curious what you think it means to be a philosopher.

GRANT: Philosophy is the extreme human presumption of claiming to be open to the whole, isn't it? And that is a great presumption. Indeed, many people say you can't be open to the whole. Now, I think that openness to the whole arose for me — and perhaps it does for many people — from the passion of astonishment. I was just astonished.

I've talked about the kind of secular liberalism that I grew up in, and that seemed to me inadequate very early in my life. This was astonishment. Because my parents were splendid people, I couldn't believe that I found their view of the world inadequate — do you see?

The war was astonishing. What I saw happening to Canada after the war was astonishing. Up to about 1940, Canada was overwhelmingly an agricultural society, with small groups of lawyers, doctors, teachers in the towns who thought of themselves as really running Canada. Now, I was part of that class of lawyers and teachers, and it was extraordinarily astonishing for me to see, after 1945, that my class was disappearing in Canada. The place of these older-fashioned teachers and doctors and lawyers was now taken by the E. P. Taylors and C. D. Howes of the world. A new Canada had arisen, and whether it was for good or ill, it was just astonishing for me.

CAYLEY: Surely Canada was dominated by a commercial élite from the outset.

GRANT: Yes, quite. But what I'm saying is that in 1940, when the Americans were not in the war and the Canadians were, there had to be a quick rising of industrialism to send arms and things — that's what I mean by C. D. Howe. You see, my family were the lower reaches of the old mercantile élite, the people who really worked for them. I have a watch, the first watch that Sir Sanford Fleming put twenty-four-hour time onto. My grandfather, who was a clergyman, worked for Sanford Fleming. Sanford Fleming is the perfect example of that mercantile class. I'm saying that a new form of capitalism arose: industrial capitalism — continental industrial capitalism — came up in 1945, and was a quite new class, wasn't it?

One thing I can't insist on enough, which is, it seems to me, absolutely central to understanding anything in this world, is that fast-moving technological change means fast-moving moral and religious change. Anybody who thinks the contrary, who thinks of technology as something outside themselves, doesn't know what they're talking about. The fast-moving changes that started in the Second World War and carried on with the decision, in 1944 and '45, to greatly integrate this country with the United States created new classes that were foreign to the class I had been brought up in. People are wrong to say that I'm a crazy old romantic who wants to go back to the past; but if they say that mine was a class that was disappearing and that that was what led me to philosophy, well, there is some truth in that — that's all I'm saying.

Now this isn't a final truth about philosophy, but just an incentive. Astonishment about being itself, about what is, is philosophy. People have said that philosophy starts in wonder; I just prefer the word *astonishment*, that's all.

CAYLEY: *Wonder* sounds more romantic, but *astonishment* suggests something that strikes the soul with great force.

GRANT: Exactly, exactly.

CAYLEY: You began to teach philosophy in Halifax?

GRANT: Yes, and here I owe an enormous debt to James Doull,[99] who is still in the Classics Department at Dalhousie. He was an extremely educated person, exactly my age. So far everything had come to me through Christianity, through the Bible. He enabled me to read Plato, and that taught me how it was possible to think rationally about God and about justice and about the things that concern us here below.

CAYLEY: How do you mean *rationally*?

GRANT: To think about them. To think about God coherently. Let me say first that the great statement for me of all modern statements is Simone Weil's: "I'm ceasely torn between the perfection of God and the misery of man" — meaning that this tension always puts the idea of God in question. But on the level at which one thinks about politics, one thinks of economics, one thinks about the institutions of education one's children are in and one is in oneself, then one can't believe in God with one side of the mind, saying that this has to do with the hereafter, while you think about the world in the kind of pragmatic liberalism that is everywhere.

What Plato enabled me to do was to see some unity between thinking about ordinary things and my belief in God. And I think this is very hard for people. Take, for example, what's gone on for centuries in Canada — people coming from agricultural areas, where they had gone to church and believed in God, coming and meeting professors who use the criticisms of the Enlightenment against this belief, and they're thrown into confusion because they can't meet or understand any of this. I wanted some way that I could think about God. It was just necessary to me, otherwise I would have been left in a totally divided state. I think this is one of the hard things about modern life. Most people are not intended for sustained thought. I don't mean this in a patronizing way — there are more important things to do, such as loving, and all kinds of things — but when a society is in as great an intellectual chaos as the Western world is, where nobody knows what anything is about anymore, then I think that this mass public confusion is terribly hard for people. With most people, their main life is not to think, and therefore they can be easily driven here and there. People speak against tradition, but tradition was what was handed over, and it was meant for most people who had busy lives to get on with, raising their children, earning their living, governing the state — doing all these things that most people have to spend most of their time on. If people do these things they aren't meant to think very much, but now that this is gone, a great requirement for thought is put upon them.

A very wise Indian said to me once as a joke — and I think it's a good joke — that the West is considered to be concerned with *right* and the East is considered to be concerned with *rite.* Now, we immediately think, Oh, how much better we are; but you know, when the West has lost its rite, in the Eastern sense, which it has, it's a position of infinite sorrow for people.

I'm not saying the end of life is thinking: I'm saying the end of life is doing what is good, and I certainly don't for a minute mean to put forward some kind of crazy inequality. I have no doubt that within Christianity everyone is equal before God. I don't think you can hold Christianity for a minute without believing this. There are inequalities that represent some truth in the world, as well as ones that represent untruths in the world, but ultimately, before God, people are equal.

CAYLEY: When you spoke a moment ago of "openness to the whole," what did you mean by "the whole"?

GRANT: It seems to me there are moments in human life, moments of very great intensity and probably to do with action in regards to other people — that is, with morality — where one asks more than a finite question. One asks, What is it all about? I want to insist that I'm not especially good at paying prices or anything like that, but this is why I have always emphasized justice. There are questions of justice that raise the question, What is the whole? And the greater the price one has to pay the greater is one's openness to the whole. Justice costs something.

One of the things that I find most difficult about modern North American conceptions of justice is that people seem to think it is without price. Somebody said that modern American liberalism is Christianity without the cross, which is a smart remark; I mean, it's inadequate but it's clever. Now, as to how the whole arises for one, let me quote someone who is, for me, a very high authority: Mozart. His account of what it is to compose is an account of being given wholes. He talks about a composition being given to him all at one moment, "all in one look," he says.[100] Now, from a quite different angle than justice, that's what I mean by whole. Then one can put this in Platonic language and speak about the idea of the good. The word *good* for me is just a synonym for the word *God*. As Plato said, the idea of the good is just the idea of final purpose. The whole is opened to one when one asks the question of final purpose. This takes us back again to justice. This is why people have always exalted the martyrs, isn't it? — because they are the people who are asked questions of final purpose in a very immediate way.

CAYLEY: In 1947 you wrote an essay called "Two Theological Languages,"[101] about the relations between Christianity and philosophy . . .

GRANT: May I say that I now think that essay is quite wrong. The great question is the relation of philosophy to revelation, or as it's been put, what has Athens to do with Jerusalem? I wrote that essay before I was aware of some of the things I just spoke to you about, when I was in a mood of exalting the language of Jerusalem at the expense of the language of Athens — rather like Jerry Fallwell[102] — and I think that is always a mistake. I mean by Athens systematic thought . . . No, I don't like *system*; *system* belongs to armies and I don't like it about thought. Careful, coherent thought is what I mean by the word *Athens.*

CAYLEY: And you feel you sold that short initially?

GRANT: I did in that essay, very much. I was on the side of the theologians who say, What has Athens to do with Jerusalem? I was very close to those people who say that you just receive revelation and that's all that is required.

CAYLEY: What changed your understanding?

GRANT: Well, first I was moved by my close friend here, James Doull, and then I thought about this in connection with the thought of Leo Strauss and later Simone Weil. But it has been my life to ask about the best way to think the truth of the gospels. That sounds very pretentious. I'm getting more and more pretentious as we go along, but what I have been most deeply concerned with in life is how one thinks the truth of the gospels. You have to remember that in any of the languages of the Bible, both the Old and New Testaments, there is no word for nature, there is no word for history, there are no words for many of the things that in the West have been found essential for thinking about the world. These are all words that come from Greece. Obviously, we don't know what life Christ may have had that we are not given in the gospels, but going to the cross is not an act of philosophy, quite, is it? There doesn't seem to be much philosophy in the gospels; and if you want to think of the gospels in relation to the rest of the world, and all that is in the world, you at least need some coherent discourse with which to think about it. This is why the theologians have used philosophy, isn't it? Christianity doesn't provide one with a *Weltanschauung* by any means. It's not that which one gets from the gospel, is it?

CAYLEY: How does philosophy supplement the gospels?

GRANT: Suppose you say that through the incarnation Christ is fully God and fully man, and that this has occurred. This may have been for some Christians self-explanatory; but if you take the argument of the Doukhobors with the Orthodox Church, and there have been endless situations of this kind, then it is clear there can be differences about meaning, and therefore philosophy becomes necessary in the pragmatic sense in which I have been talking.

Now, of course, philosophy can be an end in itself quite apart from the gospels. There are lots of wonderful philosophers who are not members of Christianity, Judaism, or Islam, who are open to the whole without accepting one form of revelation or another. Philosophy is a Western word, but there are Indians I have known whom I can only call philosophers. They don't use this word, because it isn't part of the Sanskrit tradition, but I can't think of them as anything else but philosophers. Nor do I think they are being Westernized in becoming philosophers. Philosophy, it seems to me, is something that belongs to human beings as human beings. It is something very separate, in a certain sense, from Christianity, and that makes the question we are discussing hard from both sides. It is hard for me on one side when I think of people like St. John of the Cross[103] and see that he was doing the one thing needful for Christianity; or on a very different level, when I think of somebody like Dietrich Bonhoeffer[104] and then have to ask, why does one need philosophy? Or I can look at it from the other side and ask why does philosophy need Christianity? Both questions arise for me — Why does Christianity need philosophy? Why does philosophy need Christianity? How can I be a proper philosopher if I'm within Christianity? You may be sure that many people have pointed out the difficulty. Now, both those questions I want to answer as lucidly as I possibly can, and I haven't been very lucid at answering them.

CAYLEY: When you ask, How can one be a philosopher within Christianity?, do you mean how can one be a philosopher when the answer to one's questions has already been definitively revealed?

GRANT: Revelation doesn't teach you many things, but it teaches you the end for man . . .

CAYLEY: And in that sense forecloses certain questions . . .

GRANT: Yes, and it also puts something higher than philosophy: it puts charity higher than contemplation. I think there's no getting away from this, that Christianity is in some sense a break with Plato. Now, there are all kinds of ways of uniting them, and this is what Western society at its height has been; but it does seem to me that on the question of the place of charity and contemplation in life and their respective importance, there is a break between Christianity and philosophy. And I'm taking philosophy not just as what is taught by certain professors, I'm taking philosophy as Plato.

II
THE MODERN MISTAKE

CAYLEY: I would like to talk today about *Philosophy in the Mass Age*.[105] You wrote that book after you had been living in Halifax for about ten years, and in it you remark on the transformation of the city over that period — not necessarily physically, but more in terms of the emerging corporate culture. What kind of experiences had you had living in Halifax during those years?

GRANT: I came to see that Halifax was utterly dependent on Toronto and Ottawa, and that they in turn depended on New York and Chicago, and this was a great experience for me. I really started to learn what the North American system was. I learned more when I went to live in Ontario, but at that time I was living quite simply.

The basis of that book was coming to philosophy and above all the philosopher Hegel, the greatest, most wonderful thinker of the doctrine of progress. Nietzsche said that Christianity is Platonism for the people. One could say Marx is Hegelianism for the people in the same way. And then one also has one's immediate experience. We were having lots of children then, and I was seeing who ran Dalhousie, how it was run, what it represented in Nova Scotian life, the relation of Nova Scotian life to Toronto and Ottawa life; that was living. At the same time what was basically happening to me was thinking about how Western Europe had been dominated by the idea of history, and history was most consummately thought in a modern way by Hegel. Our lives are not split up, and these two things were going on for me at once.

CAYLEY: It was Hegel's view that the truth of ancient philosophy could be subsumed in a modern vision of progress. You later concluded that this wasn't possible. How did you initially understand Hegel on this point?

GRANT: Hegel had a consummate understanding of Lutheran Christianity, which held him. He had a consummate understanding of the French Revolution. Central to these understandings was an idea that wasn't around in other civilizations, the idea of history, of human life, and human freedom making itself in the world.

The French Revolution, which was the great revolution, was based on the idea that you were going to produce a society of free and equal human beings, a worldwide society of free and equal human beings, and this is what history was about. This was the basis, it seems to me, of the doctrine of progress; that with modern science you could produce a worldwide society of free and equal human beings. Now, that was a prodigious vision and seen, I'm sure, most deeply and most completely by Hegel. Ancient philosophy had been the rational or free side of this; Christianity had brought in equality, and the two together, when they were made concrete in the world, would make possible this worldwide society of rational and equal human beings. That has been the great Western idea. The West conquered the rest of the world not only by its science but by this immense idea, and this included the notion that there was something called history that was working itself out in the world through human beings.

The great distinction of the ancient world was between nature and convention; the great distinction of the modern world has been between nature and history. Everybody talks about history, do they not? They're always making their claim to be doing something in the course of history and all this kind of thing. Now, *Philosophy in the Mass Age* was written under the domination of this idea of history. I really believed this. One always has in life a series of things battling against each other inside oneself. I'm sure that's true of all of us. I spoke previously about the last war and the sinking feeling it gave me about Western history. But still, after the war I came to believe that this idea of progress working itself out in the world was something one could believe and hold, and of course, the great thing about Hegel was that one could hold it with the Christian religion, you see? In a way you can say that, in a very unthought way, this is what the United Church was in Canada when it was a powerful institution.

CAYLEY: Because Hegelian idealism played such an important role in Canadian intellectual life?

GRANT: Yes, though intellectual life in Canada has never played a very great role. That's one thing about Canada, isn't it? What's taught in colleges about philosophy has never had much influence on the real course of Canadian life, has it? But the doctrine of progress has.

CAYLEY: In *Philosophy in the Mass Age* you speak hopefully of "the dawn of a new age of reason," and that seems to be partly founded on your experience with the young and with the freedom you see them as having in relation to tradition. I'm interested in the sources of the hope that you felt at that time, that you could use a phrase like "the dawn of a new age of reason."

GRANT: Well, I think the sources of hope — and I don't mean to sound very academic — were in philosophy. When you read philosophy in any real sense, you're asking if it's true or false, and I thought I had seen in the philosophy of Hegel a way to take all that was great in the past and reshape it as progress.

I was teaching extremely hard then; there were a lot of very fine young people around, and I saw a kind of dawning. Now, I've taught a lot of wonderful young people, and there have been great dawnings in North America at certain points. I think the whole protest against the Vietnam War was a great dawning. North America was the only place where the young people really hoped to shape a great new society. Europe had the same people in a way — there was Rudi Dutschke[106] and all these people — but not in so massive a way as in North America, nor so proud and fine a way. The phrase you quote was, of course, written long before the Vietnam War, and it may have been no more than one's first teaching, because I was astounded by the excellence of the Nova Scotians I was teaching, and the capacity for reason and thought in them filled me with hope. But I think what was basic was coming to terms with things like Marxism that I had never really thought about before, and seeing the greatness of this account of life as progress — a Western phenomenon, in which what is present both in Christianity and philosophy is carried out and incarnated in the world. And that's certainly what Hegel is about.

CAYLEY: One of your interpreters, Joan O'Donovan, has seen in that period a "restrained Hegelianism." I think she feels that there's something already present in your thought which is limiting or restraining the Hegelianism — that is, that everything you were saying in *Philosophy in the Mass Age* is not in Hegel.

GRANT: I've never thought of that before, and this is, as I say, very egocentric, but let's talk about Hegel and Christianity in this question. Let me put it this way: Christianity had talked about the purposes of God in history, if you want to use this modern language, but these purposes were always known as inscrutable. What I would now say about my thinking in *Philosophy in the Mass Age* is that those purposes were being made scrutable. There was always present in me a remembrance that what is absolutely final as far as Christianity goes is that God's purposes are inscrutable, but I fell into the temptation of thinking of life or the purposes of God in human life as too scrutable.

CAYLEY: You talk in *Philosophy in the Mass Age* about limits, and about the need for a category of evil which is absolute. Now, I know little enough about Hegel, but it seems to me that Hegel excuses almost everything in terms of "the cunning of reason" and that therefore your sense of wanting to set limits and preserve the idea of natural law is not at all Hegelian. Are there perhaps two quite different strands in your thought that you have managed to integrate for the purposes of this book?

GRANT: *Managed* is the right word [laughing]. I don't mean dishonestly managed, but I think you've hit the absolute point. I think one sees this in Marxism, and these days it's easy to see because Marxism is identified with an empire that is a rival to our empire, and therefore everybody speaks of it as a devil, and this kind of thing, which I just don't want to get *near*. But it does seem to me that Christianity, whether Eastern, Western, or Hinduism, for that matter — and I would think Buddhism too, though I know less about it — have to reject the idea in Marxism that good ends can be achieved by bad means, and I think that is already in Hegel.

This is related to the idea of limits, and to the necessity of knowing in advance that there are things one will never do, things that one can know would be wrong at all times and in all places. Modern thought has been insufficiently clear about the impossibility of good ends being achieved by bad means. The idea of limit to me is the idea of God. I don't have any conception of what God could mean except an imposition that is not tyrannical, an imposition that one imposes on oneself, that there are certain things that one can know in advance should never be done. Later on, when I was trying to think this all out, people kept saying what nonsense I was talking, that if you had a man walking around the city with an atomic bomb and only his child knew where he was, it would then be all right to torture the child, and so on. And I came upon, it seems to me, a very lucid example: the judicial condemnation of the innocent. The point of a judge is to decide whether people are innocent or guilty of particular crimes; if a judge, knowing somebody to be innocent, condemns him, there's an example of something that must be always and absolutely wrong. It seems to me a very good example of a limit that is imposed always.

CAYLEY: What about your other example of the atomic bomb and the child. Can you answer that?

GRANT: No. But I think these hypothetical questions are the kind that the people who are governing us, political human beings — and I mean *political* as a good word — must think about all the time, mustn't they? They must think hypothetically about what they're willing to have done or not done. Don't you think that unless people who are in the practical world think of this all the time, gradually they will be willing to do anything?

CAYLEY: Yes, I do. I'm just stymied by your example. How would I decide what to do in those circumstances?

GRANT: Yes, it's terrible, but I only gave the example to say that even if you said yes to torturing the child there was still such a thing as a limit in the judicial condemnation of the innocent, because that is something that should *never* happen. People are always asking for examples of limits that cut across the idea of progress, and this seemed to me a very small but very clear example.

Practical people have to think about such things all the time. Until recently, one of the great things about the era of progress was its cutting down of torture. We can surely agree that this was a great thing. Now, in our era, torture has come back in a big way, and by people who believe in progressive ideas. Somebody who was very wise said to me once that in modern society there are two classes on whom the decency of the whole society turns: the doctors and the police. This was said to me about twenty years ago and one now sees how true it is every day. The limits these two professions impose on themselves are fundamental to the possibility of a civilized society, are they not? But I wasn't really thinking about all this yet when I wrote *Philosophy in the Mass Age*. I was still enormously engrossed in seeing the greatness of Hegelianism and its epigones, like modern, progressive liberalism in the United States, or Marxist progressivism elsewhere. So, though I agree with you that I didn't go altogether that far, I was still very engrossed.

CAYLEY: I see what you mean, and yet I still think that your critique in that book of the inadequacies of Marxism, as of the American pragmatism of John Dewey and William James, is quite penetrating.

GRANT: Well, I guess this is there just from Christianity, but I hadn't thought it through, really. It may be just vanity that makes one write anyway. In this case the book was written as radio lectures for the CBC. I was very poor at this stage, with five children and a sixth one coming, and I suppose it was more money than vanity. But it may have been that I wrote before I was ready to say anything of importance. That happens in life, does it not?

You have to remember academic salaries were very poor in those days. I was very scared about being able to cope with my responsibilities to my children, and then, because the Russians put Sputnik up in the skies, academic salaries soared and all that worry disappeared. Economic worry has been very central in my life since I got married. You have responsibilities to children; you have to see that you have enough to eat and a place to live and get them educated and so on. I just saw the end of the Depression — and my dad was a very prosperous schoolteacher — but I remember going out to work one summer for Canada Packers. My father had gotten me the job. It was in a small place; there were twelve people who worked there for practically nothing. One day one of the big bosses from head office in Toronto came through, and I remember suddenly seeing that the other people who worked there would all have liked to have killed him. I realized that. They couldn't do anything. Even though I was cushioned from the Depression by my dad having a good schoolteaching job, that always remained with me. So, when I suddenly found myself earning three thousand dollars a year with five children — and I thought professors were really something — I had to get going.

The Depression is something about North America that people often don't remember very much. They forget that intellectual life in the United States in the 1930s was entirely dominated by Marxism because of the Depression. It's a quick-moving society. Now the United States is the head of a great empire around the world and there is some poverty, but incredibly little. Lenin is not a character I have the greatest admiration for, but there is one true thing that he said: There is no real proletariat in England; the proletariat for England is really in the Third World. Well, that is true of North America today to a great extent.

CAYLEY: Turning back to *Philosophy in the Mass Age*, what subsequently happened to the views you put forward in that book?

GRANT: Again, the details of personal life and intellectual life are blended. First, my home town was Toronto. I wanted to be close to my mother and people like this, so I returned to Ontario and saw what had become of Toronto.[107] At the same time, the contradiction you clearly expressed about *Philosophy in the Mass Age* was becoming clearer to me, and I found that contradiction in political philosophic terms wonderfully expressed by Leo Strauss.

Leo Strauss was an immigrant from Germany, with a great German philosophical education, and he brought that to the United States. Almost sheerly by accident I started reading his works, and I began to see the contradictions in modern progressivist thought, which I had not previously understood. And that is the central issue — that there were contradictions in this progressivist thought, particularly Hegel's thought, that I came to see.

CAYLEY: What was Strauss saying that made you see this?

GRANT: Strauss in a very wise way limited himself to modern political philosophy. He didn't write very much about modern science and modern mathematics; he concentrated on modern political philosophy. And this limitation was a great help to me, because if people try to say too much, you never learn anything from them. Strauss had a great controversy with a very famous Hegelian Marxist.[108] In it he spelled out what he thought was inadequate about modern purposes, namely that our purpose, our great political purpose, is to build a worldwide society of free and equal human beings. Now, this is clearly a great purpose. Anybody who doesn't think so hasn't looked at the world at all. But Strauss came to the conclusion, for reasons that are difficult to state quickly, that the pursuit of the worldwide society of free and equal people — what I call the universal and homogeneous state — will lead to tyranny. And since he regards tyranny as the worst form of government, he concludes that this great end that was expressed at its best in the French Revolution is not a proper end for people to pursue. Of course, this worldwide society of free and equal people is deeply related to modern science, which issues in the conquest of human and nonhuman nature.

Strauss thinks that the great progressivist vision of Hegel expresses itself politically in two ways: first, that all human beings are open to be philosophical; and second, that philosophy and science will take the place of religion. To both these statements Strauss says no, and he thinks these are basic statements within Hegel. They are statements that are necessary to understand why Hegel believed that a worldwide society of rational, free, and equal human beings was possible.

CAYLEY: Strauss speaks of what he calls a "lowering of the sights" in modern political philosophy after Machiavelli. What does he mean by this?

GRANT: Strauss thinks that the height for human

beings — that is, the highest good for human beings —
is lowered by political philosophers for what seems to
them a good reason: if you lower the sights, you'll be
able to achieve a better society. In the English-speaking
world you see it in these great thinkers, Hobbes and
Locke. The end of life, in their thought, becomes comfortable self-preservation. The end of life to the ancients,
the height of life, was openness to the whole, and in
that openness, to know the highest good, which is God.
Strauss says somewhere that the desire to overcome
chance, which is in modern science and then modern
political science, was probably the reason why modern human beings became oblivious of eternity. This
lowering of the sights was of course done for the very
best reasons — to build a good world here on earth.
The higher sights, openness and inquiry into the highest purposes of man, were thought too difficult. These
higher purposes were overcome first by the English,
then by the French, and last and probably most completely by the Germans. This led to a lack of desire for
eternity, which is man's greatest need. The attack on the
ancients began as the overwhelming attack on Aristotle
that you find in the first modern scientists. In political
philosophy it began with Machiavelli and then
worked itself out thoroughly in the English, the
French, and finally the Germans. This lowering of the
sights has, to Strauss, done something very terrible to
Western man.

What came to me at this period was the thought
that perhaps the Western experiment, the experiment
that had gone on since the seventeenth century in both
natural science and political science, had been a mistake. That is the great central thought that I have tried

to think; and it's very hard to think, you know, because we're all brought up within the idea that the Western experiment is supremely good and something that has to be taken out to the whole of the world. This doubt of the Western experience has certainly been the central idea of my thought.

CAYLEY: I have a curious reaction when you speak so bluntly as to call the civilization of the modern West "a mistake." I think very few sophisticated people today would say they believed in progress, and yet confronted with this blunt idea, I still tend to bristle and think, how could it have been a mistake?

GRANT: This is why one must think very carefully and write very hesitantly. I'm very hesitant in talking this way. I don't believe in retreats from the world, for instance, except retreats so that one can better live in the world. People have said about me that I am a pessimist, and that is a word that I really object to. Now, as you know, the words *optimism* and *pessimism* were invented by Leibnitz, who said optimism means that it's the best of worlds and pessimism means that it's the worst of worlds. But if you believe in God you must be an optimist — mustn't you? — in any real and fundamental sense. Just because one is not sanguine about a particular civilization, Western civilization, granting some of the great things that it has done, just because one is not sanguine about the results of its natural science and political science — science in the sense of knowledge and thought — just because one is not optimistic about those . . . I mean civilizations have come and gone, have they not?

A lot of the great questions are quite frankly just beyond me. I am quite certain in speaking about God, for instance, but I am not at all certain about whether God is a creator. I can believe in the eternity of the world very easily. That's why I admire Strauss and these people who have thought about the immediate teaching about politics of the great modern thinkers, because on some of these ultimate questions, I wonder if the people who think that they can understand them aren't just deluding themselves. Certainly I cannot understand them. I'm beginning slowly now to understand more about what it means to say that God is love, and this is connected to my understanding of the beautiful, but there is still so much more. The supreme figure in all philosophy said that the philosopher is the being who knows that he knows not, and people who don't know that they don't know are very dangerous.

CAYLEY: When you speak of modern political philosophy's attack on the ancients, what is it in classical philosophy that is being attacked?

GRANT: One of the great turning points of the Western world was when Socrates decided that he wasn't going to be so interested in the stars and the planets and the motions of the earth and this sort of thing; he was going to be interested in man, in human beings. This was a great turn-around. Political philosophy grew out of the idea that the most important thing for the philosopher to do was to think what was the best regime under which human beings could live. The two main people who came out of this were Plato and Aristotle, and this has led to a great division in the West. The Catholic West to a very great extent accepted Aristotle, both in natural science and in political science, and this is one of the reasons there is such a great difference between the Eastern church and the Western church. The Western church fundamentally chose Aristotle; the Eastern church fundamentally chose Plato. As far as my own thought goes, I have fundamentally chosen Plato; but though they have important differences, they also have a great deal in common. One of the strange things about life is that the very greatest can be at the beginning; and in this sudden awakening to what political philosophy was, both Plato and Aristotle agreed that the first job of thinking people was to think very clearly about what constitutes the best regime for human beings. This was a sudden, wonderful moment of outbreak with Plato and Aristotle, and their fundamental agreement — because, you know, their disagreements are fairly narrow — about what constitutes the best regime held European thought from there on, until the break occurred. This break, both in natural science and what one could call "moral science," really happened in the seventeenth century. And I have been concerned above all with what that break was in moral science, rather than natural science.

CAYLEY: In what way do Plato and Aristotle agree on the best regime?

GRANT: The best regime is certainly first and foremost the city. The mark of the city is not that everybody knows everybody else, but that everybody knows everybody else at no more than one remove. I may know you, David, and you can tell me about somebody called Jim, whom I don't know. They certainly believed that these regimes are higher than imperial regimes, very large regimes. For instance, Aristotle said something which I think is very clever about the barbarians — and by barbarians he just means the people whose words all seem to begin with "b," non-Greeks. "The barbarians," he says, "know freedom but have no civilizations; the Babylonians have civilization but no freedom; Athens has freedom and civilization." I think a statement like that very deeply sums it up. The ancients are very shrewd about the best possible regime in any given circumstances. They are not at all utopian; there may be circumstances that make the very best regime impossible. Utopianism, with its hope for enormous changes, is a much more modern phenomenon.

The other thing which I think is the core of Machiavelli's attack on the ancients — to go back to your previous question — arises around technology. The ancient political philosophers thought that there had to be very cautious and careful control of inventions; some led to good, some led to bad, and they had to be very cautiously controlled. They recognized that if you live in a city you are going to have to defend yourself, and they believed that where there are human beings, there will be war — a very hard doctrine and again I don't know whether it's true or not. But they did not accept that this need to defend oneself must lead to unlimited invention or to an unlimited relation between science and invention.

Now, before we go any further, I want to make one thing perfectly clear about modern technology: my wife and I would have been slaves, with six children, if we hadn't had a washing-machine and stove and electricity. This is something that *must* be admitted and must be seen with clarity, along with what I call "the oblivion of eternity" that went with it. To talk about this, one has to see so many things on so many sides at once, and I don't want to jump around and seem to imply that we can all go back to a world that included slavery.

CAYLEY: On the question of the best regime, it's obviously central in Hegel, for example, and in all modern thought, that the ideal can be realized. What was the teaching of classical political philosophy in that regard? That is, did they believe that the ideal could be realized, and if so, how?

GRANT: One rather tricky little point I would like to make is that the ancients had no word for *ideal*. The notion of the ideal as opposed to the real comes essentially from Hegel's great precursor Kant. But if I take your question to be, Can the best regime be realized?, then I would say that the ancients weren't prodigiously optimistic. The city was seen as fairly self-contained; that is, not requiring a vast amount from other people economically. I think both Plato and Aristotle probably saw the best possible regime as a mixture of democracy and the rule of landed gentlemen.

But this shows you why I won't leave technology out of the picture for a minute. It is inconceivable that we moderns would think this way. I don't mean that modern political philosophy was a product of modern scientific technology. They went hand in hand, as coming from the same thought, and that thought was quite different from the ancients. Each helped the other. Some people in a rather dead era like ours think that all that matters is technological development, but technological development to a very great extent took place because of these political ideas. They go together. I don't think that one can finally separate natural from moral science, and this is presumably how they're initially thought together by these very rare occurrences, these philosophers, like Hegel, who take into themselves all that is happening in the modern world at a certain moment. I wouldn't for a minute call myself a philosopher in this sense. I would call myself a really quite competent teacher of philosophy and quite competent student of it, but I don't pretend to be somebody like that any more than I could ever be like Mozart.

CAYLEY: Strauss says in *What Is Political Philosophy?* that the classical political philosophers felt that, human nature being what it is, the best regime could only be actualized by chance. He goes on to say that the attempt to overcome chance is one of the foundations of modernity. What does chance mean in this context?

GRANT: If I put a spade down in my garden and found a gold piece there when I was planting a geranium or something, that would be chance. The moderns aren't so foolish as to think that you can eliminate chance or necessity from human existence, in that sense. I think what the ancients saw, when they established cities all over the Mediterranean world, was that this required people wise enough to ensure that the cities did not become greedy, that the cities did not become overly warlike, and yet were not so soft that they were just conquered immediately and incorporated into empires. These are all great chances, aren't they? That's what they mean. And when I talk about political philosophy, one must remember that the very word comes from the *city*, the *polis*. Western society starts above all with two giant deaths, doesn't it? — the death of Socrates and the death of Christ. And Plato and Aristotle, because of the death of Socrates, knew with a great deal of clarity that cities were liable to be the enemies of philosophy in the sense of contemplation of the whole. A great enmity to philosophy was seen in Socrates' death. And in that sense, they thought it was by chance that the very height, this openness to the whole, this contemplation of the whole, could be present in any city.

Something that has cleared my mind a lot is Socrates' assumption that all human beings are religious. He was always making religious oblations to the religion of the city of his day, polytheism — a very beautiful and wonderful religion. It's interesting that the greatest modern philosopher is a polytheist. It seems unbelievable, but I think that Heidegger is an authentic polytheist. Socrates believed that no society could exist without religion. Religion is very much a matter of tradition, of what has been handed over, and he distinguished religion from philosophy. Philosophy was a kind of openness to the whole beyond the traditional religion, and he recognized that this high philosophical life that existed for a moment in Athens but soon went down was very chancy. I think the ancients were just enormously aware of how much all our lives are ruled by chance.

I always think of something that happened when I went to college back in England after the war. I said, Oh God I won't go to this party, and then, No I've got to go to this party, and I went and I met my wife! I mean, if you don't think life is dominated by chance . . . and this has been the great event of my life, certainly. I don't think you can eliminate chance from life; but if you've ever had a sick child you're glad there is interference with chance. I certainly wouldn't be alive at this moment if there wasn't modern medicine, which is the supreme practical exemplar of interference with chance. To talk as if interference with chance is not necessary is obvious nonsense. But the question of how far it should go is another matter.

CAYLEY: You're saying that we overcome chance for moral ends, and yet Strauss seems to say that by dominating chance we destroy the possibility of excellence. Why does he think that is the case?

GRANT: When a society is entirely directed to the overcoming of chance, it gives human beings the sense that they are the owners and masters of the world, and we all know what that has led to. It also seems to prevent them from knowing that they are essentially owned by something beyond them. I don't mean owned as slaves — here all language fails — but that there is something beyond the passing that we do not measure and define, but by which we are measured and defined. That's my language, but something like what Strauss is saying. And I think there is enough evidence in the modern world to say this is true. One of my difficulties here is that I'm not very keen on personal language about the Deity, not because the modern women's movement makes me want to call God her or him, but because in this matter I'm fundamentally a Platonist. I don't want sub-personal language, but I don't like personal language about the Deity, because personal language is another modern language that I don't altogether like. We used to talk about our person as meaning how we were dressed, how we appeared — that's how people would have used the word in the past. It was something fairly external about them. Because the soul has disappeared, it's now come to mean the very essence of man, his personality, and I don't like that way of talking about man, that's all.

Simone Weil once said this fantastic thing: that she preferred to call Providence "chance." And there she is saying, I think, that one mustn't take Providence as something that is scrutable. One of the things that one is always annoyed by in Christian believers is when they say something is providential. How in hell do they know? I mean if He's doing it there, why isn't He doing it in Abyssinia? I think that the idea that Providence is scrutable is a terrible idea. It's a blasphemy. It's a cause of unbelief.

CAYLEY: To continue with Leo Strauss for a moment, he sees modernity as having evolved in several "waves." What is the sequence that he sees?

GRANT: He's talking about modernity as political philosophy, as thinking about human beings; and the first wave, which centres on Machiavelli, was incarnated in England in John Locke, who as you know was basic to the foundation of the American Constitution and the English Constitution. This was the first wave of modernity — the lowering of the sights to comfortable self-preservation. Then came the second wave, which he sees originating with that strange and fantastic genius Rousseau, and he sees that second wave as essentially the discovery of history. This is what is worked out so beautifully in Hegel and Marx. He sees the third wave as originating — and this is personifying it — in Nietzsche and people like Heidegger, who see with great clarity that history is meaningless, and yet think it is all there is, and who attack the equality and social democracy of the French revolutionary progressivist wave. Nietzsche no longer believes in progress, and he's the beginning of what I take as existentialism. All other origins of existentialism are minor compared to Nietzsche.

Leo Strauss lived in the United States and I wouldn't go there during the Vietnam War, but the only time I did see him, somebody asked him a rather silly question: when he would have liked to have lived. And he said, "Now." Why? Because, he said, the most complete and wonderful account of the whole had been given in Plato, and the most complete and shattering criticism of that account of the whole had been given in Nietzsche. He could not have reached either of these, he said, but because he lived now he could live in the presence of both. I thought that was smart because certainly one couldn't have thought Nietzsche for oneself, I don't think.

CAYLEY: I was certainly amazed when I read Nietzsche, something I was led to do by reading *Time as History*, your 1969 Massey Lectures.

GRANT: My wife always says I should never have talked about Nietzsche. People have said — Strauss indeed said — that Nietzsche had a right to think what he thought, but it was dubious whether he ever should have written it down, and it was even further dubious that he ever should have published it. My willingness to read Nietzsche and to teach him is that now, a hundred years later, everybody is surrounded by popular Nietzscheanism, or popular existentialism, at every point; therefore, they better read the source of it with his intoxicating rhetoric.

CAYLEY: Did Strauss believe, or do you believe, that it would have made the slightest difference whether Nietzsche had published or not? Does a philosopher actually originate ideas or just somehow articulate what is already present?

GRANT: Well, this takes us directly on to Heidegger. To Heidegger truth means bringing something out of concealment — that's what truth is. The question is whether this prodigious, brilliant, lucid attack on social democracy — on Rousseau and Marx — was good for people to hear. One of the Church Councils — I think it was the Council of Orange — said it was necessary to believe that God cooperated both materially and formally in evil (this is Aristotelian language), but said it must never be preached from the pulpit. Today, you just have to go to the movies. Everything is open, and it's for this reason that I'm willing to discuss it. Whether Nietzsche ought to have brought out of concealment certain things that for the political health of societies it might have been better not to have brought out is another matter. Plato's only really practical dialogue about what kind of regime he wants is his *Laws*, and in it he says the council must argue *very* carefully with people who do not believe in God. Then they must be brought back about six months later, but if they aren't finally brought to belief, then they must be expelled from the city. And he goes that far, you see, because he thinks that natural religion — that is, what is to him true religion — is necessary to the city. People are given a lot of space; it isn't very cruel, as people have often made out about Plato, it's just that finally, if they cannot be convinced by people in the city, then they have to leave.

CAYLEY: Nietzsche criticized Strauss's second wave of modernity as represented by Rousseau and Hegel. How had they criticized thinkers of the first wave like Hobbes and Locke?

GRANT: Hobbes and Locke had said that human beings are not naturally social, but had taken for granted that human beings are naturally rational. Rousseau made the gigantic step of saying that human beings are neither naturally social nor rational, that their rationality developed in time. Darwin was the person who expressed this in modern scientific terms with the doctrine of evolution, but Rousseau had said it with outstanding clarity a hundred years before Darwin. Rousseau said that human beings were not by nature rational, but that rationality was something they developed through the accidents of history, and he said that Hobbes did not understand this.

Rousseau was a great contractual theorist, like Hobbes. His most famous book is *The Social Contract*, a great revolutionary book that would have been by Robespierre's bed all through the Reign of Terror. And he agreed with Hobbes that men are not naturally social, which I don't think is true, but then he made what seems to me a prodigious step for the West by saying men are not naturally rational. Rousseau agrees that contract is the basis of society, but he raises the question of how men get sufficiently rational to make a contract in the first place. He says this in an early discourse called "A Discourse on the Origins of Inequality," which I think is actually a key document for understanding Western European history.

I'm not sure Rousseau has always been well understood. I mean, if you take Bertrand Russell, in his *History of Western Philosophy*, you would think that Russell would be above all attacking the Christians and people like Thomas Aquinas; but in fact, the person he turns on with particular fury is Rousseau, though he doesn't get near what Rousseau was saying. You know people think of Rousseau as an artistic, rather silly sort of person, and indeed he had a wild and very strange life; but when he gets down to saying something, clearly and carefully, he's a genius of a very high order. All the German thinkers like Kant and Hegel come out of this. Kant said about Rousseau that what Newton had done for the planets Rousseau had done for the human questions. He was as great a genius as this. If somebody like Kant can say this, he's not being foolish. Now, again, whether Rousseau was right to bring this prodigious attack on the ancients out of concealment is another matter — but he did it and did it consummately.

CAYLEY: Classical philosophers had held — you say this somewhere — that "being is eternally identical with itself." What is implied in the view that being is itself historical?

GRANT: It's an obvious academic escape from a prodigiously difficult question, but the nearest I can come to answering your question is to quote Hegel. In one of Hegel's very great books, *The Phenomenology of Spirit*, he says at the beginning that he is no longer going to think of God as substance but as subject. Now a subject is never identical with itself, insofar as we can think about something and we can think about ourselves thinking about it and we can think about ourselves thinking about ourselves thinking about it, etc., etc., etc. Subjectivity and objectivity are the great language of modernity, and I think they have helped with all the wonderful sides of modernity. This gets us back again to Mozart. The English word *object* comes from the Latin for something thrown away from us.

When you see something objectively, you hold it away from you. It is not something you can love. This is why I brought in Mozart earlier — because of the beauty of the world, and because his art is the very form to me of the beauty of the world. Now, anything beautiful cannot be for us an object; anything loved cannot be for us an object. *Subject* just means thrown under, doesn't it? It means the self which is underneath all statements from the self. This language has been remarkably useful to modern natural science and to modern moral science, but it's a language that I now want to get rid of. And this property of being as "identical with itself," it seems to me, is something that Hegel is getting rid of, in talking about God as subjectivity.

CAYLEY: Whereas for Plato . . .

GRANT: For Plato the good is there in its supremacy whether we know it or not. Now we're getting into realms where I have no right to speak and don't really understand; but obviously when we say "God is love" we cannot think of God as a simple, self-identical unity; this was why the doctrine of the trinity arose — to face this question.

CAYLEY: What I've taken from what you've said is the idea that if being is identical with itself, then nothing we can do will change it.

GRANT: Quite.

CAYLEY: The question I would then have is whether Meister Eckhart, for example, when he says, "God cannot know himself except through me," is saying the same thing as Hegel or something quite different?

GRANT: He's saying something *very* close to Hegel, isn't he? Very, very close to Hegel. And presumably it's because he said such things that this very great mystic has not been beatified. I'm not just talking politically. I think all the great German philosophers were deeply influenced by these earlier German mystics of which there is none greater than Eckhart. I am closer by nature to mystics like St. John of the Cross than to these German mystics, and I imagine the resemblance of what you've quoted from Eckhart to what I've been saying about Hegel is exactly why.

I've thought mainly about political philosophy, as you know. The questions you've just raised are the fundamental questions, but I have wanted to know the nearer and household questions before I moved on to them, and I'm just beginning to move on now.

CAYLEY: Well, the household questions are hard enough, so let me ask you a final question about Leo Strauss and the idea of history. One of the words that bears a lot of weight in his thought, and in yours, is historicism, and I'd like to ask what is meant by it.

GRANT: Well this will again connect directly to Heidegger, because Heidegger is incomparably the supreme historicist; he has thought it to its absolute depths. At a simple level, and that's how I always start, otherwise you just lose touch with sense and immediacy, historicism is the exact opposite of Platonism. Historicism is the belief that all profound thought arises from and is dependent on a particular dynamic context in human life, and to understand the thought one must understand that particular dynamic context. Platonism is the belief that thought can transcend its context. Historicism at an even simpler level is the belief that everybody's opinions about everything are historically determined, and in that sense it seems to me that it goes very deeply with existentialism. It was Nietzsche who thought historicism first and most prodigiously. Now, clearly, any presumption that has held modern Western thought as universally as this assumption has in the last 150 years is not going to be shallow or foolish. Nothing that holds large masses of thoughtful people is going to be just nonsense, and I now think historicism is the fundamental assumption of all social science.

I used to think that the division between judgements of fact and judgements of value was the assumption that dominated modern social science. I still think it is an extremely important assumption. Everybody left, right, and centre is always talking about "your values" and "my values," etc., etc., but I don't think it is as important as the historicist presumption that we are all in a particular dynamic context, and our thoughts are determined by that particular dynamic context. I think that's just dominant.

One of the central ways to understand historicism, which of course I want to speak against, is through Nietzsche's attack on Socrates. Socrates, Nietzsche says, couldn't face the fact that the world is an abyss of chaos, and therefore he turned away in fear from this abyss of chaos and pretended it was rational. I had a friend in Cornell who was writing his thesis on Nietzsche's portrait of Socrates, and it so disturbed him he went out one night in New York and lost seventeen thousand dollars at poker. It was one of those games where they told him, "In a week a leg will be broken and we up the ante from there." All his friends had to come up with this money, but quickly! That shows you how difficult the question of Nietzsche's portrait of Socrates is [laughing].

III
LAMENT FOR A NATION

CAYLEY: When did you move back to Ontario from the Maritimes?

GRANT: I went to Ontario in 1960, the year John F. Kennedy came in. I went in order to take a job at York University, and had to resign from that job because they wanted me to use a textbook that was very anti-Christian, which I obviously couldn't do. So I worked for a year for Mortimer Adler and Maynard Hutchins,[109] and then got a job at McMaster and stayed there for twenty years.

CAYLEY: What was the dispute over the textbook about?

GRANT: I was the first person appointed to an academic position at York, and it was a question, from my perspective, of their having lied to me. I found out later that they were under the control of the University of Toronto, and they were asking me to use a textbook that made fun of Christianity and of Platonism. So I just refused and resigned, but it meant I was in Toronto on a loose end for a year.

CAYLEY: You have already spoken of your anxieties about supporting your family — resigning must have been an act of some courage.

GRANT: Yes, well, I have a very courageous wife.

CAYLEY: [Laughing] You take none of the credit for yourself?

GRANT: No, not very much.

CAYLEY: What was the text?

GRANT: It was a text by a man who taught philosophy at the University of Toronto, Marcus Long, and it was a textbook that I simply refused to use, because to me it perverted both Christianity and ancient philosophy. So that was that. I then got a nice job at McMaster, after a year. But in the meantime I worked for the Encyclopaedia Brittanica. I didn't want to leave and go and live in Santa Barbara, so Mr. Adler and Mr. Hutchins let me do the work in Toronto.

CAYLEY: Shortly after your resignation from York you wrote an essay called "Religion and the State," which reflected on the place of religion in civic life. Later, when that essay was collected in *Technology and Empire*, you added an introduction in which you described your earlier belief that such an essay could make a difference as a folly.

GRANT: Well, I think the position wasn't very sensible, was it? It was unaware of the modern era at a certain level.

CAYLEY: What was your position in that essay?

GRANT: I think the position was that it's necessary to distinguish between the public religion and the true religion and to recognize that any good society is in need of some kind of public religion just to exist. Now, I'm just about to publish a book that includes an essay in which I praise Sartre.[110] I think Sartre is a lesser philosopher, and a bit of a bastard. He tried to have Céline, a very great artistic genius, killed. But I am including that essay to show what folly one writes in the past. Otherwise it appears that one had things all worked out in advance, when in fact, one's thought does deeply change. To take a most absurd comparison, when Mozart learned counterpoint, the very greatest works of his genius, his piano concertos, started to change. I think the same is true of Shakespeare; some of the earlier plays are less good than what followed. This happens with lesser people as well as the very great, and I think lesser people should admit that they have written some stupid stuff in their time. "Religion and the State" is not one of my favourite pieces.

CAYLEY: You think now that you were foolish to try to make the case for a public religion at that time?

GRANT: In Canada, neither French nor English started with the Jeffersonian division between church and state that the Americans had. I'm not saying that they believed they were identical, and I would also add that it's only in the Christian West that you have had this division at all. One of the things that is difficult for people to understand about Khomeini's regime is that in Islam you don't have this division — whether for good or ill being another matter. What I am saying is that I don't think I sufficiently understood how much Canadian society had been cut off from its roots and had become essentially accepting of the Jeffersonian position. I think I was just unaware, as one is so often unaware of what is going on around one; this is one of the facts of human life that one must never forget: that all of us move around thinking we understand reality when we don't, in the most immediate sense.

CAYLEY: So you are saying that your ideas were not so much wrong as naïve?

GRANT: Yes, exactly.

CAYLEY: What was the effect of the Vietnam War on the shape your thinking took during the 1960s?

GRANT: I think the Vietnam War was an atrocious war on the part of the Europeans, undertaken to maintain their power right around the world, first by the French and then later the Americans, who I take to be an epigonal civilization, or part of Western civilization more generally. I think it was atrocious to do that so far away.

I was living in a place very near to where bullets were being made to be used against the Vietnamese. The students who were protesting the war knew I was quite a strong Canadian nationalist and these very radical students came to me to support them in a large protest against government policy. I had admired very greatly one person who I thought was a great gentleman in Canadian politics, Howard Green from British Columbia, Diefenbaker's foreign secretary. He had continually stood up to the United States, and this changed when the Liberals came back in. Therefore, I was quite willing to support this protest by these left-wing students. I liked them immensely as human beings. They were very fine, splendid human beings.

They had had success with protests at the American Consulate and things like that. But then they proposed more extreme actions that I was unwilling to carry out. For instance, they wanted me to just lay my body in parliament and have it removed by force, along with a lot of them who would do it, too. Now, I was unwilling to do this. It may have been just that this was very alien to my nature and it may have been fear, I don't know; but I was unwilling to do it. If I look for a reason, I would say it was because the Canadian parliament seemed to me then an institution that gave us more independence against the United States than the corporate world I knew in Toronto, and therefore I refused this. The students were very bitterly angry and went on with the protest, which didn't come to much, and they ceased to be interested in what I was doing.[111]

CAYLEY: And yet you continued, I think, to have quite a following among the young — perhaps not with this specific group . . .

GRANT: This group was mostly at the University of Toronto. I think this book I had written called *Lament for a Nation* had had an effect on some of the young, and therefore I continually saw people coming and going, etc. I mean if one ceases to communicate with coming generations, one is half dead, and I don't like being half dead.

CAYLEY: You were also briefly involved with the New Democratic Party around this time, weren't you?

GRANT: Yes. It's interesting to remember that both Pierre Trudeau and I contributed essays to the volume that was published at the time the NDP was founded. Mine was just on what is proper about equality in a society.[112] But I swore to myself that I would never have anything more to do with the NDP when they agreed with the Liberals and voted Diefenbaker out of office, after he had done a fundamental thing. He had attempted in his wild and crazy and strange way to do something fundamental about Canadian independence over nuclear arms. So when the NDP voted with the Liberals against people like Howard Green, I never wanted to have any more to do with them.[113] I recognized, and I think this is very true about French Canada, too, that North America is a society that is altogether going to be run at the local level by the bourgeois, and I found more real nationalism in the bourgeois, in the nationalistic bourgeois, than I did in the NDP, who were so full of ideology. But politics are very tricky, aren't they? For example, I really admired Lévesque for putting up Monsieur Duplessis's statue. Politics are not quite as easy in the modern corporate, capitalist state as the NDP seems to think.

CAYLEY: What had been your relations with the NDP before that time?

GRANT: The invitation to contribute to this book came out of the blue. I had not been involved with the CCF, but was rather inclined to vote for them to help things that seemed to me intrinsically good, like state medicine. I take it for granted that it's just crazy in a modern industrial society to be against a national scheme. So I had inclined to vote for them on these grounds, and then they were producing this book and they asked me to write something about equality — I think because of an earlier book I had written. I used to meet Trudeau at these meetings all the time. These things are all very complex, and I am so full of the idea of fate and so full, with Simone Weil, of the idea of *amor fati*, the love of fate, as a virtue one must attempt to have. Canadian politics seems much farther away from me now, but it just enraged me that after Howard Green had really tried something, and Diefenbaker had really stood up against a great fellow-populist hero like Kennedy, here were the NDP voting them out in the name of a servant of the United States, like Lester Pearson.

I suppose if you don't call the Bible a book because the Bible is a set of books, the greatest book that's ever been written is Plato's *Republic*, and I see Plato's *Republic* to a great extent as the attempt of Socrates to remove political ire from these young people. Therefore, I think I may have been too taken up with political ire in my love of Diefenbaker.

CAYLEY: What was your relationship to John Diefenbaker?

GRANT: Well, I had been so moved by his refusing to be pushed around, as I had been by his foreign secretary, Howard Green; and when I met him, like many other people, I found something in his wild and maniacal way that was very lovable.

He once gave me his account of his meeting with Kennedy. And with Diefenbaker, one thing you may be sure of was that he would exaggerate but never lie. He was a good Baptist. So Kennedy said, "You have to take the nuclear missiles," and Diefenbaker said, "Well, we're not going to," and Kennedy said, "We won't give you loaders for wheat to China . . . we'll cut off loaders and we'll cut off your selling wheat to China." Diefenbaker said, "We have a loader company," and Kennedy said, "It's American-owned." And

Diefenbaker said: "We'll take it over." And finally he said to Kennedy, "You're not in America now, President Kennedy."

What I admired in Diefenbaker was just the apotheosis of straight loyalty, loyalty without great intelligence, but loyalty. There's something noble about loyalty, unless it's to something very evil, and Diefenbaker's loyalty was to good things. Most people have to live by loyalties, don't they, in a deep sense, and Diefenbaker, for all his craziness, was full of this.

CAYLEY: How often would you have seen him during the years he was in government?

GRANT: Oh, I didn't know him at all. That is, I had known him through a friend I went to school with, who was Edna Diefenbaker, the first Mrs. Diefenbaker, whom people have said silly things about. I think Edna was great for Diefenbaker because where the second Mrs. Diefenbaker just praised him and flattered him, Edna was a very intellectual woman, much more intellectual than Diefenbaker, and she would just say, "Oh, that's nonsense, John." I think Diefenbaker would have done much better in power if the first Mrs. Diefenbaker had been with him, you see, because she was smart enough to stand up to him. The second one just flattered him.

So I'd seen him years before, but I never saw him when he was in power at all. I think he often did very silly things in power, no doubt about it. I mean, his being a Baptist made him pick the most God-awful French-Canadian lieutenants because he had all this prejudice — stupid, foolish prejudice — against Catholics, which made him very poor as far as French Canada went. This is all past history, Baptists and

Catholics. But I admired him in his fall and saw a lot of him afterwards. He asked me to write his life, but I couldn't. It would have taken years, and I couldn't just drop my work. I like both, but philosophy is incomparably more important to me than politics.

Canada has had some crazy prime ministers. If you take, in order, Bennett, a person I have some admiration for; Mackenzie King; then you get a great deal of sanity with Mr. St. Laurent; but if you take Bennett, Mackenzie King, Pearson, Diefenbaker, and Trudeau, you've got a wild lot. I'm not talking about the psychiatric ward, but you know, you could practically be there. If people think Canada's dull, just look at those people; some of them I think did good things, some of them did very bad things, but they weren't high in sanity, I don't think.

CAYLEY: But surely King, for example, during the time he was prime minister, seemed the model of sanity, and we only found out about his peculiarities later?

GRANT: Well, you see, in my youth, King was in and out of our house a lot because my uncle, Vincent Massey, was national chairman of the Liberal Party, and used our house to meet in. King was charming, but you know, in personal behaviour, just a nut.

CAYLEY: And that was evident to you as a boy?

GRANT: Pretty soon, yes . . . do you remember John Grierson, who was head of the Film Board? One of his chaps got a picture of King and Grierson thought it really got King down to the ground — as the "sissy gangster," Grierson said. So he sent it to Mr. King and asked him to sign it for him. King always insisted that he be given all negatives of pictures of him, and he made Grierson put in writing that there was no record of this picture. King was pretty rough, I think.

CAYLEY: And he recognized that this picture some-how showed it?

GRANT: Yes, it didn't show the bland fellow, ad-mired by all these bland members of the United Church who in those days loved the Liberal Party. King didn't want them to think they were run by a . . . well, as Grierson said, "a sissy gangster."

CAYLEY: Getting back to *Lament for a Nation*, you said a moment ago that the book was conceived in anger. Some critics of your book have said that its polemical elements pull against its philosophical elements . . .

GRANT: Well, I'm quite willing to say that they know where they can stick it [laughing]. I think it's a dread-ful loss for human beings when they can no longer take part in the practical life of their society. This is what I was saying earlier about the *polis*, this is what was meant: that everybody in the society should have a chance to take authentic action — that is, activity that really matters. And that's why I react to people saying that philosophy takes one away from politics. I think anybody who has lost the ability to take part in the politics of their society has lost something very ter-rible to lose, and in great empires like the North American and the Russian, one loses it, and this is surely a great condemnation of the modern. Even if they take part foolishly, it belongs to human beings as human beings to take part in the life of their society.

CAYLEY: So you're saying that your lament was as much a lament for the loss of politics as a practical activity as it was for the loss of Canada — or perhaps that the two are the same?

GRANT: The same, yes. The possibility of building in

the northern half of this continent something different from the great empire we share it with is gone, and to me this certainly was a loss. Why should we disdain direct, immediate, practical politics? I mean, if you read the greatest of all philosophers, Plato, he's full of talk about Creon and Pericles. The heart of Plato is his attack on Pericles, because Pericles had made Athens an empire, and empires are always greedy. This goes right to the heart of Plato. Philosophy should certainly be trying to understand the incomparable and difficult logical puzzles that we are all concerned with, but it also must be more than that. This was what Socrates' life, and his great turnaround towards human beings, meant.

CAYLEY: In *Lament for a Nation* you meditated on the relationship between what you called "love of one's own" and "love of the good." How do you see that question today?

GRANT: Let's talk of love of one's own. What is most one's own in a way is one's own body. One has to get on reasonable terms with one's own body and love it, in a certain sense — this was certainly something I had difficulty with coming from the world in which I was brought up. But people who don't pass beyond that to the love of something that is of more universal significance are hardly anything. There may be much in one's own that isn't intrinsically lovable, and much in it that *is* intrinsically lovable, but I think it's a good start for nearly all people. I think one of the things about Protestantism that was very dangerous was the idea of the rule of the saints, the idea that everybody could become a saint. I think the saints are those people who have passed beyond loving their own, in the most prodigious way. But most of us have to start with love of our own and do the best we can to move beyond that.

Nationalism, or I suppose patriotism might be a better word, is a love of one's own. My granddad and my dad taught at Queen's, and a child of mine went to Queen's. I don't think Queen's is a very great university by any means — there are all kinds of flops and failures — but in some sense it's my own. This gives me more affection for it. Now, I'm not saying this should close one's eyes to failures and flops in oneself. It's the same with one's children. There is just no doubt that it's easier to be just to one's children than to everybody else. One can fail at that and not be just as a result of what used to be in the old days called "spoiling" children, but I think generally that there are much worse things you can do to children than spoiling them. In other words, I think that justice appears for people first in their own. People who are savagely bitter about their own, but love universal justice are often, to me, dangerous people.

CAYLEY: The label that was most often given to you at the time we're talking of was "Red Tory." Is that a term that you were ever willing to acknowledge yourself?

GRANT: No, it's not a term I like very much. I think it is true that, if you take the CBC, it was founded by Bennett; if you take probably one of the great saving instruments of Ontario, the Ontario Hydro — for all its faults — it was put through by Sir Richard Whitney. The Tories have done a lot. I think what the term points to about me is my great resentment of the identification of the word *conservative* with the right of individuals, of private individuals, to make money any way they want. The freeing of private enterprise is precisely liberalism. I think Canada, to exist on the northern half of this continent, has to preserve certain indigenous institutions. Now, this is not to speak against people who are good entrepreneurs — that would just be silly — but I think the language has been totally turned around when you identify the loosing of free enterprise at all costs as conservatism. I'm not speaking here as a socialist. I think the proper balance is extremely difficult and extremely complex, but I think in the Canadian situation there are certain institutions which we need and which we should know that we fundamentally need. It is very clear — and this is talking quite outside partisan politics — that if you don't have a national broadcasting system in Canada, and if you don't have a lot of public things of this kind, Canada will just cease to exist altogether, even what's left of it. I don't like the word *Red Tory* for this very much; but you know, if one goes into the public world, anybody can call you anything, and I think quite rightly. I'm not trying to stop them.

CAYLEY: But you're saying that your concerns related more to national survival than to some a priori ideological position you were taking?

GRANT: Of course.

CAYLEY: In preparing to talk to you, I looked up an article in *Canadian Dimension* called "Horowitz and Grant Talk." It was published in early 1970, and it had a little italicized preface that made you sound like a bit of a hippie. I thought this nicely expressed the affection of the New Left, and of the young generally, for your work. Now it's clear, at least in retrospect, that at this time you were moving towards a more tragic view of the fate of Western civilization, so I suppose that you must have viewed the high hopes of the young with a certain pathos.

GRANT: I admired greatly from a distance the fact that large numbers of young Americans wouldn't go along with the Vietnam War — and I saw a lot of these people coming and going in Canada, and I just liked them. Almost my favourite remark of the twentieth century is Abby Hoffman's account of liberalism: "God is dead and we did it for the kids." I liked very much their seeing how deeply American liberalism was an ideology. They saw what I had always taken for granted, that this was a great empire that had won the last war and was held together by an ideology that was necessary to corporation capitalism, and this was a great liberation for me. These were not necessarily the best people to get things done politically — I think it is often the small-town bourgeois, like Daniel Johnson,[114] who are great in politics — but these people seemed to me to be saying the truth.

I didn't like the pretensions of the Kennedy regime very much. They seemed to me to be exalting a certain kind of Americanism and trying to pretty it up with Jackie in the front row. I didn't like this. And that these young people could see these immediate social questions with such practicality and sense made me love them — that's all. Leo Strauss once said, and I think it is *the* best thing ever said about teaching, "Never go into a class without thinking that there is somebody in the classroom who has a greater intelligence and a nobler heart than yourself." That remark is so good that it just reduced me. I mean if you *don't* like the young, for God's sakes don't be paid a lot of money to teach them! Or if you're bored with it. I mean many people might be bored. I'm at the point where I want to retire, I don't want to teach at the moment. I want to write and think and read things that I've never read, and at sixty-seven I have a right to do that. But if one is teaching the young, in all their variety and all their difference, one must love them or else, what the hell, why do it? That's obvious but often forgotten; it's been forgotten in the mass multiversities. But a person like Strauss did not forget it, that's why he had a prodigious influence in political philosophy and within the Jewish community in the United States — because he loved the young.

CAYLEY: Well, I don't want to embarrass you but I think you've had an influence for very much the same reasons.

GRANT: Thank you. I *do* think this is a terrible difficulty of these mass universities. I was educated in universities that were reserved for a particular class, and therefore were wrong in that sense, but at a place like Oxford, there was more real education than in the mass multiversities.

CAYLEY: *Lament for a Nation* announces the end of Canada, at least as a certain kind of historical community. What is left in your view?

GRANT: Well, one can make it too absolute. I think there are realms of Canadian life in which people can still make indigenous decisions. I think it has become manifoldly clear that, in the big decisions, we are more and more closely tied to the American empire. When you think of the civilization of southern Ontario, its way of life may have slight differences but it is not unlike the suburbs of Chicago in some ways. Now, we do not have a large population that was brought unjustly to North America as slaves. Our people have different origins and came as immigrants. We have always the question of seeing that there is fairness to them, but we don't have that great division that's in the United States, between a large black population and a white population that originally used them as slaves.

I'm all for maintaining what differences we have. There are certain things we can do; but, as far as political sovereignty goes, we are pretty well as close to the Americans as the Poles are to the Russians, and, except for the French Canadians, the textures of our societies are not that different. In Central Ontario particularly, we live in an advanced, industrial-technological society as much as Chicago or Buffalo do. I mean, I used to go alternately with my children to the Buffalo zoo and the Toronto zoo, since we were equidistant from Buffalo and Toronto; and though there is a great difference between the two societies, and Toronto is the great capital city of Canada, which makes it quite different from Buffalo, in a certain sense the way of life is not fundamentally different.

CAYLEY: *Lament for a Nation* had a curious, even paradoxical effect. You presented it as a lament, but among younger people like me, it helped to galvanize a new nationalism.

GRANT: Well, I thought that was just excellent. I think it's great that there's new nationalism in Canada; I think it's great that there has been new nationalism of an authentic kind in Quebec. One of the things I found difficult about Trudeau was his attack on authentic French nationalism. I have found the coming-to-be of French life in North America just wonderful. It has produced the art that has most moved me — and I mean by art not just painting, but movies, music, poetry, etc. I see no reason why one shouldn't try to do what one can to see that there is an authentic difference between Canada and the United States. All I was trying to say, and I think the Cruise Missile decision made this clear,[115] was that on very big questions, very great pressure can be brought, and if you have an economy which is out of your hands, then those decisions are going to be of a certain kind. That's all I really meant.

CAYLEY: Do you feel yourself to be part of a living community in Canada today?

GRANT: Well, Canada, as we've seen in the last few years, is divided in many ways. One of the things that really rocked me and made me want to get out of Ontario was when Trudeau ran his election campaign against Lougheed;[116] I felt that this was a division of a terrible kind. But generally, I can't imagine being anything else but a Canadian. I just can't imagine.

I remember an old railway worker, a man who drove engines for the old Hamilton-Buffalo Railway, a small railway which goes down to Buffalo. I used to go fishing with this man, a very nice man, and I said, "What do you really think of Buffalo?" And he said, "Oh, a great place. I've got a great place to stay there overnight." But then he said, "I wouldn't want to be buried there." That's about what I feel about it [laughing]. Now, this is quite apart from the political stuff — my fear of the American empire and my hope that in some small ways Canada can sometimes mitigate the damage it does. For instance, I am fearful of what the American empire may be planning about Central

America,[117] and I like to think that Canada could stand aloof from some of it.

A big thing to remember at my age is that the world won't end when I die. A lot of people need to learn this, and I think one tends to learn it as one gets along. I take for granted that Canada is an entity that will go on; I hope it is able to maintain an indigenous culture; I hope above all French Canada can have a culture that is somehow different from the rest of North America. And I mean by culture quite a big thing — I don't mean only art galleries and rock concerts, I mean the way in which people live in all sorts of towns and all sorts of situations.

Let me just tell you a story which illustrates the extraordinary world we've lived in. When I was leaving Ontario, I went to see my mother's oldest friend, who was ninety. You know the geography of Toronto; you know Bloor and Bay. This woman was a great horse rider and had lived at the corner of Bloor and Bay, and she told me the hunt had once met at her house. Fast technological change means different worlds, doesn't it? And in this sense, it is very hard for human beings. Immense, quick-moving technological change is easier for the smarties, and I would include myself, but for many people it's very hard, isn't it? I don't notice the hunt meeting at Bloor and Bay any more. Do you?

IV
THE THIRD WAVE

CAYLEY: Earlier we spoke briefly about what Leo Strauss calls the third wave of modernity — the philosophy of Nietzsche and Heidegger. You have paid close attention to both these thinkers, and I would now like to talk about them in more detail.

GRANT: Well, I don't know if you think this is totally redundant, but let me say first that the great public fact of this century has been the end of Europe, caused above all by the English and the Germans fighting. And since we all live in an English-speaking society, it's become more difficult for us to look fairly at the Germans — this great and wonderful people — because so much of our effort in this century has been to smash the Germans.

Certainly German society has been a great ambiguity in the Western world, and more so in the contemporary era, as distinct from the whole modern period. The greatest thinkers of that era have been Germans, and I would say the two supreme thinkers have been Nietzsche, about a hundred years ago, and in our present time Heidegger, Nietzsche's great epigone. It seems to me that Nietzsche is the person, the first person, who expresses modernity at its fullest: he says it is the end of the age of reason, and he proclaims this as a great event. He says that the age of reason in the West was expressed essentially through Christianity and through the Greek philosophy that penetrated Christianity, and out of that came modern science. He calls the modern scientists "the gravediggers of the age of reason" because modern science has taught us that we cannot look at the world as if all that is is rational. Modern science has made it impossible for us to believe that what is is ultimately reasonable and proceeds from the divine reason. One only has to think for a minute of Darwin to understand what he means; Nietzsche thought Darwin was a very great genius — which indeed he was.

Nietzsche claims that the age of reason was an aberration in the history of the world; the height of the world, for him, was Greek tragedy. Greek tragedy was the understanding that life is an abyss of chaos and greatness is to be destroyed — the greatness of tragedy is seeing the beautiful destroyed by the chaos of existence. He agrees with the Greek tragedians that life is a chaos. Then Socrates came along and, according to Nietzsche, he could not face the fact that existence is an abyss of chaos, and so Socrates became the great seducer of mankind into the age of reason. Christianity was just a popularization of the age of reason, Platonism for the masses.

Nietzsche sees himself as the proclaimer of the end of that age and he recognizes that the results of that end might be simply negative. Therefore, he says, Europe is transfixed with what he calls "nihilism," nothingness. He uses the image of the three animals. The age of reason and Christianity is the age of the camel that carries around its hump on its back. The gravediggers of the age of reason are represented by the lion — the lion who brings down the foolish camel that had to carry around the great hump of Christian belief on its back. The lion has destroyed the camel but still lives in the desert, and that is nihilism, the great lion. And then the third animal, which symbolizes what Nietzsche is trying to do as well as those people who have passed beyond all this, is the child who is able to live in the world in innocence and joy without the camel hump of belief and without the desert of the lion. And, you know, it is not surprising that Herbert Marcuse, whom we identify with the left, was a student of both Heidegger and Nietzsche. His picture of how we're going to move into the innocent world of polymorphous sexual pleasure is not so far from Nietzsche's child, in a way. I've never thought of this before this moment, but one thing that was strange about the left during the 1960s and 1970s was the fact that Marcuse was always thought of as a Marxist. And he was in a way, but he was a Marxist who had studied with Heidegger, and was penetrated with Nietzsche. The 1960s and 1970s were not only penetrated with Marxism, but with something much, much deeper:

the greatest critic of Marx who ever lived, namely Nietzsche.

CAYLEY: Was Nietzsche even aware of Marx?

GRANT: I don't think he had ever read Marx. When I say he's the greatest critic, I mean that the foundation of Marx is in a greater thinker than Marx, namely Rousseau, and Nietzsche is certainly the supreme critic of Rousseau. The equality of the social contract and social democracy is just part of the decadence of nihilism to Nietzsche. Certainly nobody was ever a greater critic of egalitarianism. He pictures people walking around in nihilism saying, "We are all equal, we are equal before God," and Nietzsche just says, "But this God has died." Egalitarianism came essentially from Christianity, and yet the people who believe it now don't believe in what sustained it, therefore it's bound to go — do you see?

CAYLEY: In your explication of Nietzsche in your book *Time as History*, you also stress his psychology of the instincts, and the way it prefigures thinkers like Freud.

GRANT: Well, as you know, when Freud read Nietzsche he said, "Everything I have said is already there." Freud is a kind of epigone of Nietzsche — he was a gentler man, not as great a man, and therefore he didn't see the consequences of what he said so clearly as Nietzsche. But with Freud, what is central is that the human being is no longer seen as the rational animal, he's seen as an *id*, an *ego,* and a *superego.* And what is fundamental is the *id.* It was Nietzsche who first called man an "id," an "it," and claimed that what is fundamental to us is instinct. Instinct is impersonal; that is its "itness." And the idea that man is finally instinct has come to be believed in the modern world; this is why Freud in the past was popular in the United States. This is extraordinary! People don't like the Nietzschean consequences of this, but in the United States they all believe — do they not? — that the definition of man as the rational animal is no longer true, and that what is actually fundamental about man is instinct. Reason is just a little extra for calculation and for getting us comfortable and doing technology and things like that. So this comes back to what I said about modern science being a gravedigger. Modern science, which was an enormous rational activity, destroyed the idea of man as the rational animal, as the animal who is fundamentally called to a destiny which is more than instinct.

CAYLEY: When you say modern science did this, are you saying this was implicit in modern science from its very beginnings?

GRANT: Well, take the example of Darwin. He shows in *The Origin of Species* that man can be well understood, as everything in science can be understood, as the product of necessity and chance. The idea of *good* or *purpose* need not come into it. Modern science, whether of the Newtonian kind or the Heisenbergian kind, explains everything without the idea of ultimate purpose — does it not? — and if you can explain everything without the idea of ultimate purpose, then there is no ultimate purpose. I know people have said that we can opt for God without any reason; but if you can explain everything without the idea of ultimate purpose, then men will cease to believe that there is any ultimate purpose. This is why positivistic people — scientists — always become fundamentally existentialists in their lives, because existentialism is just a taking over of the consequences of modern science and the claim that you can explain everything without the idea of purpose.

CAYLEY: So you're saying that nihilism was implicit in science from the beginning, despite the belief of many early scientists that they were acting in a religious spirit. I know Leibnitz said that Newton's God was no more than a retired engineer, but Newton himself described the universe as "God's sensorium," and thought of himself as something of a prophet.

GRANT: Quite, but he explains the motions of the planets without the idea of purpose. Very early on Plato says that your explanation for the motions of the planets will determine everything you think. People now ridicule ancient science, and I'm not saying that a sane person can believe some of it any more. It's only a person like Heidegger who can say that ancient science is as true as modern science, meaning that it's all historically determined at every point. I don't think modern, sane people can look at ancient science and say it's true, but I think they also have to look at the consequences of a nonteleological science because the consequences for man of a nonteleological science are nihilism — and this is what Nietzsche saw with overwhelming clarity first. He just saw it, and he thought it was a good. He faced the end of the idea that man had purpose, and he accepted the new idea that the universe as a whole was purposeless and that our purpose was to be master of it. But he says in the last book of *Zarathustra*, "the hour approaches — the hour when I shiver and freeze, which asks and asks and asks, Who has heart enough for it? Who shall be the lord of the earth?"[118] This shows how seriously Nietzsche took a question that we can think of with some directness today in terms of atomic weapons. He is asking who will deserve to be the master of the earth, and I would think that everybody on earth has enough sense to hope that somebody will deserve to be in charge of these extraordinary bombs, which have come from this mastery. Perhaps somebody will. I don't want to be a doomsayer; I hope to God that people will arise who can deal with this.

CAYLEY: When you gave the Massey Lectures in 1969, you chose Nietzsche to illustrate the idea of what you called "time as history." What did you mean by that expression?

GRANT: Well, to compare it with other visions of time, the archaic vision of time was of a cycle. People not only lived in the cycle of the year but in the cycle of the ages, and this was very deeply part of the ancient world — that Socrates had taught and died in Athens an infinite number of times — do you see? In the West there is the idea of a beginning of man. It begins as the idea that man was created, and it becomes, in its modernized and secularized form, the idea of man having a great purpose in time, a purpose that reaches its culmination, as I said earlier, in a worldwide society of free and equal human beings where history will be realized. You see it very clearly in Marx, don't you? History begins in scarcity, scarcity produces class struggle, and out of class struggle the purpose of man is to produce a classless world without struggle. I think one means by history that the human race as a whole has a beginning, and a purpose coming out of that beginning which will be fulfilled in the future.

CAYLEY: And what do you think is the origin of that idea within Western civilization?

GRANT: God, that's difficult! I would say fundamentally its origin is the Bible, both for Jews and for Christians — that is, the whole Bible. Here were these people who were chosen by God and went into the wilderness, and then into exile, and are going to come back to Jerusalem — God has a great and immediate purpose for these people. Then Christianity comes into it and says that this purpose has been realized in Christ. I think this is the origin of the idea in the West, though the word *history* itself is Greek.

Today, most of the Western world is made up of secularized Christians and secularized Jews. Do you remember — this is just a joke, but I think it's a very good joke — a Spanish person saying to Bertrand Russell, "You're a Protestant atheist and I'm a Catholic atheist and we have nothing in common" [laughing]. There is a lot of truth to that. The modern West seems to me to be taking this biblical vision and secularizing it — that is, eliminating God from it. So history, as Rousseau formulates it, becomes the idea that man comes to be by accident, but then it is his purpose to realize a rational society here on earth.

Everybody these days talks about the difference between American liberalism and Marxism, but they're utterly at one about this purpose, aren't they? In political terms, at the moment, their purposes seem to be in disagreement, but in fact, they both believe that their proper end is the building of the society of free and equal men here on earth. This explains, in a sense, the agreement of the Americans and the Russians to smash Europe, doesn't it, because certainly one ideology that didn't believe in this end — and I don't want to say a good word about it — was national socialism.

CAYLEY: That presumably is why men like Martin Heidegger, and even briefly Carl Jung, initially felt some sympathy for national socialism, before they were able to see the atrocity that was entailed.

GRANT: I know less about Jung's politics, although I'm a great admirer of him, but in Heidegger's case I think it was clear that he disliked the capitalism of the West and the communism of the East, and thought both of them would destroy what is noble and great in the world. Therefore he thought that national socialism might be an alternative. Heidegger got out in 1934.

CAYLEY: Before we talk further about Heidegger, let me ask another question about time as history. Is what Mircea Eliade calls "the valorization of time" essential to Christianity, or is there another way to understand it that does not involve a progressive incarnation of divinity in the world, a church that embodies this incarnation, and therefore, an idea of good overcoming evil in history. Is that Christianity itself, or is it an aberrant reading of it?

GRANT: Well, I think it's an aberrant reading of it, in the sense that you have to distinguish here between what we would call Western Christianity, which is what you've described, and Christianity itself. Western Christianity is one moment within Christianity, just as one could say that particular forms of Chinese Buddhism are single moments within Buddhism, but there are perhaps greater moments elsewhere. I have no doubt at all that Western Christianity made some great errors in its origins, and here — and I say this with great hesitation because he is a genius — I blame St. Augustine. I think it was Augustinian Christianity that shaped both Catholicism and later Protestantism and in turn led to this extreme secularized form of itself as progress. I have no doubt that Christianity is true, and therefore, I think it has to be reformulated. Western Christianity is, in a sense, over in these Augustinian forms, and it has to be reformulated, getting rid of this Western interpretation of it, which has led to these strange modern phenomena.

CAYLEY: That's a fairly breathtaking prospect, when one thinks of what is involved.

GRANT: Well, I can't look at Christ and say he is not the truth. I think many, many people in the East, for example, most followers of the Vedanta, or what we call Hinduism, would look at Christ and say he is the truth. They have no difficulty with that. The problem has been this procrustean, triumphalist Western version of Christianity, which led Western civilization out into the world thinking it could do anything it chose to other civilizations, and which became even more terrible in what it did to other civilizations when it was secularized. I think it may be a wonderful, wonderful thing for Christianity to purge itself of this triumphalism. It doesn't seem to me to threaten Christianity itself, or to threaten Christ. I mean, how could you? It's like saying you could threaten Gautama! Do you know what I mean? [Laughs]. When something has been, it has been, and there it is in all its radiant beauty. You can threaten things along the way, but not the thing itself, can you?

Do you remember dear old General MacArthur out in the East? One of the funniest things I ever heard was him saying, "The communists are going to destroy God." [Laughing]. They're not! They're not! They may do many things but they're not going to do that. This is what belief in God means, doesn't it? There are long eras of horror and terribleness where what is supremely beautiful may be eclipsed, but it cannot disappear from man. That's all. That's what faith is, isn't it? It's a strange language to use, but God is not mocked.

CAYLEY: This is very interesting. So you are saying that you feel that some new expression of Christianity is in the offing.

GRANT: In a sense, but nobody who has their brains about them at all can predict the future in any detail — where it will come, or how it will take place. I am willing to say about the future that God will not be mocked. But nobody can tell whether the bombs are going to go off or not. One hopes, one prays that they won't, but one doesn't know what will happen. I mean, one can predict, I think, that certain steps will lead automatically to tyranny and one can say that tyranny is an evil to be avoided at all costs, but anybody who thinks they can predict in detail is talking through their hat.

CAYLEY: Something that impressed me very much in *Time as History* was your discussion of the language of "values." This is something generally taken for granted — obviously we have values — but you reveal this language as an innovation occurring first in Nietzsche's thought.

GRANT: It seems to me that Nietzsche is clearly saying there are no inherent purposes in the world. What people had previously meant by "good" was what anything was fitted for: a horse was good if it could run fast or pull. Good was what we were fitted for, or what we *are* fitted for. That implies purpose. It's good for human beings to breathe; that was *good*. This was the old language. Nietzsche no longer believes that there are these purposes; the purposes have been destroyed. He wants a new language to express how we decide what we should do, and therefore he substitutes for the language of good what we are fitted for, the language of value.

Nobody has ever been able to tell me what a value is. If somebody asks me what an apple is, I can tell them what an apple is. No one can tell me what a value is. It seems to me an obscuring language for morality once the idea of purpose has been destroyed, and that's why it is so widespread in North America — everybody talks about "our values." And of course it's very funny that in North America this language is used by every onward and upward fellow. Clergymen talk of values. Everybody talks about values, night and day, when they're trying to make pious, secular sermons; and yet it comes from the greatest enemy of all this, Nietzsche. The language of value is above all the language of Nietzsche. It is what is left once you have eliminated the idea that there are purposes that intrinsically belong to being, like breathing. The ancients called thinking a good because it belongs to human beings to think, that is their nature. The language of value was just a substitute because that had disappeared. And I think it's just comic that the great and supreme originator of it is somebody the people who generally use it would not think they liked.

CAYLEY: So values are willed meanings.

GRANT: Yes. You cannot look at human life without some idea of willing and choosing and freedom; but in the ancient world these ideas of willing and choosing and freedom were seen in terms of the purposes that were given to man in the world. The central thing was to know those purposes and then one had the freedom. Once you have gotten rid of the universe of meaning, then everything becomes our making, our willing, our choosing; freedom becomes a radical freedom, as it is in existentialism, either/or in the face of the meaninglessness of the world, and I just think that's crazy. I think it would be silly to say that we haven't some freedom, that we don't have some choice, and certainly we need to will things, but existentialism cuts these choices off from any meaning in the universe as a whole. This is why all the existentialists are so full of the language of choice and will. The idea of values disguises existentialism within an apparent platitude. It prevents people from thinking about matters they should be thinking about.

CAYLEY: It seems to me that trying to reveal what is within common words is one of the main ways in which you teach. For example, in your essay "The Computer Does Not Impose on Us the Ways It Should Be Used" you take apart this sentence word by word in order to reveal what is actually implied in this platitude.

GRANT: Heidegger has a wonderful phrase, that language is "the house of being." Language is the way what is appears, the way it comes to us. Now, I think the difficulty of the Western world is that that house has become a labyrinth; there are so many conflicting languages about that it is no wonder people are in a crazy state about it. One way of speaking, for instance, that I find extremely difficult is the language of subject and object. When people want to say something is very profoundly true, they say it is "objectively true." But if you look at what is meant, as I said earlier, the word object implies that what is true is what is thrown away from us and held away from us so that we can force it to give its reasons. I think we ought to try to get rid of all the impurities of language that are now present everywhere.

One good thing about the old linguistic education was that it trained people early in inflected languages so that they became at least fairly conscious about the words they used. Now, linguistic education has been set aside because the only education that's taken seriously is scientific education, and I think that has been a sad thing for man. Something even sadder, I think, is when the greatest truths of human life can be expressed in number and not in language. As a Platonist, I am an admirer of mathematics, but I think that when mathematics becomes the way the most important truths are expressed, something of very great consequence has happened to the world.

CAYLEY: On this question of the purification of language, you seem to be saying that words have become treacherous because they carry meanings of which we are unaware. Perhaps this is what you meant the other day when you said that the Western tradition had become opaque to itself.

GRANT: It's so epigonal in the sense of having so many different and conflicting things from the past and trying to use them all. One sees this, I think, very deeply in the United States. The people I have some sympathy with about abortion are atrocious about the possibilities of nuclear war, and I find this extremely hard.

CAYLEY: Earlier in our interview you described Martin Heidegger as the consummate thinker of our age. Why?

GRANT: In his first great book, *Being and Time* — and there you have historicism right in the title, don't you? — Heidegger describes man as a being towards death. He says that human beings, insofar as they are conscious, are the beings who at every moment of their lives know they are going to die. Death is a temporal event and he is saying, I think with enormous clarity, that the centre of the modern world is choice, anxiety about death, and extreme individualism. All thought arises from the concrete, dynamic situation of the individual. This is what he says in *Being and Time*, and what I have called historicism. Now, I would say — and this is just my judgement — that since his experience with national socialism and his experience of the war and the smashing of Europe in the war, all of his later thought has been an attempt to escape from this historicism. When I talk about historicism I think of it as just an expression of existentialism. Existentialism is the heart of it; and when you think of the philosophic movement called existentialism the rest are nowhere compared to Heidegger. In a certain sense, Sartre is just a plagiarist of Heidegger. They're all little people who've just borrowed bits from Heidegger.

For Germany, existentialism was intellectually what national socialism was politically. I'm not saying that Heidegger was trying to free himself from guilt or anything — that's not Heidegger at all. He had other reasons for trying to say what the limits of existentialism are in his writing since 1945. Right after the war, when he was prevented from teaching in Germany by the allied forces and the French were longing to see him, the first thing he wrote was a letter to a French friend, called "A Letter on Humanism." There he ex-presses most wonderfully his dissatisfaction with existential-ism as a category and says he wants to try to go on thinking. He doesn't say that this great and wonderful book *Being and Time* is wrong but he says he wants to say more.

I'm trying to express this in a spirit of fairness to Heidegger because he's been so abused in the Western world. This was a very great genius — I have no doubt at all that he is *the* great philosopher of the modern era. For myself, for instance, nobody has spo-ken so wonderfully about what technology is, and this goes beyond any question of agreement or disagree-ment. Heidegger has seen what the modern phenomenon that we call technology *is*, and seen it with prodigious attention. I mean modern in the sense that there wasn't anything like what we call technol-ogy in the ancient world. There was technique, and there were arts, but technology is essentially a modern phenomenon, and it is to me the overwhelming phe-nomenon. Heidegger expressed this in a marvellous way when people asked him about capitalism and communism, and he said that capitalism and commu-nism are just predicates of the subject technology. I think that is true. They make a difference; they are predicates and they are very different predicates. One can speak very profoundly against communism and, indeed, speak very profoundly against capitalism and their different vices; but I think Heidegger has seen that the essential event of Western civilization at its end is modern technology, which is now becoming worldwide.

CAYLEY: Heidegger, in a very beautiful passage, says that we're "too late for the gods and too early for being." "Being's poem, which is man," he says, "has just begun." So "we must be claimed by being, we must be willing to dwell in the nameless." And this reminds me of your own insistence that we must be willing to really experience the darkness of our time, and listen for what you have called "intimations of deprival."

GRANT: I have to say that, for me, this is like talking about Mozart: I am honoured when you say I share anything with Heidegger, but here one is in the presence of genius I could *never* be near, and I must say that. Heidegger does say that "we're too late for the gods," but he also said towards the end, "Only a god will save us." Now, in the Western world, if you use an article before God, you're not talking about the god of the Bible, who is just God. You're talking about gods, in the sense that Apollo was a great god; and I think Apollo *was* a great god, and not just, as we now say, a "myth." Now, I think it is indubitably true that Heidegger is in some sense reaching for polytheism again. When he says we are too late for the gods, he does agree that we are too late; but in a way he is hoping, because he thinks that polytheism, the return of the gods, would be a wonderful thing.

I can't really speak about this without coming back to technology because it seems to me he is speaking about passing outside the position where everything is an object and our relation to it is to summon it before us to give us its reasons. What he means by "being here" is very close in a certain sense to the ancient tradition, expressed not just in Christianity but in India, and in a different way in China, and the Mediterranean world. He is speaking against a view of life in which we are totally summed up in technology, in which all our relations are relations to objects which we summon before us to give us their reasons. He's speaking against everything being controlled, and in favour of waiting upon what is. We must not stand before what is in the relation of subjects who want to control objects. We must be open to what is and wait upon it. This is not so much said in *Sein und Zeit*, where he just lays down existentialism with consummate, extraordinary brilliance, but in the later works where he turns to the very great German poet Hölderlin. The poets are those who listen to what is. This is the point of his quotations from Mozart. It's all the language of participation in the later Heidegger, in his attempt to say not that existentialism is not true but that one must pass beyond it. I think he was very appalled by the existentialist movement and its silliness.

CAYLEY: He quotes from Hölderlin the line, "Where the danger is grows the saving power also." He seems to feel that in our extremity a god will appear, because the nature of the extremity opens us to being. Is this a view that you share with him?

GRANT: Yes, certainly, if one says that this polytheism is in some sense within Christianity, and all I mean by within Christianity is allowing the gospels to be present and allowing philosophy to be present. So I share it with him, but I have to make the qualification that I think Heidegger has in a very deep way — though there are things that say the opposite — said no not only to the details of Western Christianity but to what seems to me always true of Christianity. And I don't want to say yes to this.

One of the interesting things about Heidegger, and something which I think is very central, is that all the previous great German philosophers had been in their origins Protestants. Many of them later forsook it, but they were in their *origins* Protestant. Heidegger is the first very great German philosopher who was in his origins a Catholic. He was going to be a Catholic priest, though he left it a very long time ago. His origins are in Aristotle, and he is, it seems to me, the greatest commentator on Aristotle who has ever lived. But my origins are not philosophically in Aristotle, they're in Plato, and I want to be careful that this separation between the eternal and time, which is so central to Platonism, is maintained, and I'm not sure it is maintained in Heidegger. That's why I'm being cautious.

CAYLEY: In what sense is this distinction not maintained in Heidegger?

GRANT: Well, this is a queer language to use, but whatever Christianity may be, it cannot get away from the crucifixion. Whatever Christianity may be, one sees here the just man being most hideously put to death, and this means to me that in Christianity there is always not only the presence of God but also the absence of God. I would say that this is central to Christianity, and that all the talk about what it is and what it isn't has often been an argument between the presence and the absence of God. Now, my question is how much the absence of God is maintained in Heidegger, and how much the absence of God is maintained in polytheism. I want to be very careful because the very substance of what I have thought about anything would go if I couldn't believe in the absence of God. And I'm not sure that this is maintained in Heidegger. This takes us to Simone Weil, who understood the absence of God with consummate genius.

It may be slightly opportunistic, but what I have learned from Heidegger is the meaning of technology. Nobody has written about it comparably or in such wonderful detail. Beyond that, I haven't really gotten that far with Heidegger, but I am inclined to think that the absence of God is not present. That's immediately talking in a contradiction, but emphasis on the absence of God seems to me to be necessary for Christianity and for anything which attempts to be true.

CAYLEY: Your calling Heidegger a polytheist reminds me of a passage I recently ran across in a book about William Blake by Kathleen Raine, the British poet. In this passage she calls Blake a Christian polytheist, something I would have thought a contradiction in terms before she put the idea in front of me. What is your own view of polytheism?

GRANT: Well, I have thought a lot about what Apollo was for the Greeks, and I certainly lack sympathy for that side of Christianity which in the early Christian days wanted to destroy the vestiges of paganism. Christianity in its early expressions often spoke against the polytheism of the ancient world, and I think that's nonsense. But I am unwilling to speak about this because I don't know enough. There is a popular modern Catholic theologian whom I think little of, Karl Rahner, and he had a brother, Hugo Rahner, whom I think a lot of. He wrote a book called *Greek Myths and Christian Mysteries*, which I think is awfully good on this, seeing the relation and bringing them together. Now, I would be utterly on that side, but I'm not saying that I know what a god is because none has descended to me. I do know with very close Indian friends, who are very wise people, that they do not think polytheism is simply something that exists in Indian religion as a useful thing for the simpler masses of India. They think it is something much deeper than that, but what it is I do not know. I think it would be very fascinating to know.

I can understand why the early Christians demolished many of the things around them that were good, but I think it was tragic. There is a story of a ship — and this is well authenticated — travelling between Greece and Italy; it passed an island which was supposed to be completely uninhabited and the mariners heard a great chorus wailing, "Great Pan is dead." I never speak against Christianity as such, but one can speak against the actions of particular Christians, and I think the sheer savageness of the early Christians' attack on paganism was unfortunate. Mind you, the pagans had been quite savage to them and there was much reason. The beginning of St. Augustine's *City of God* is an attack on the old Greek religion, as found in Rome. It had become very decadent by the time of Rome — I don't mean decadent in the sense of sexually loose or anything, I just mean that it was a tired-out old religion by this stage — but I think in the change much good was lost.

There is in Islam and Judaism this bare monotheism,

which makes me hesitant about their accounts of poly-theism. It's very strange that Islam and Judaism should be politically at war now because I find in both of them the same thing, something I am frightened of, the over-whelming power of this very bare monotheism.

V
THE WESTERN FATE

CAYLEY: You have spoken of your debt to Heidegger on the question of technology. Were you also influenced by Jacques Ellul?

GRANT: Ellul was a rather different matter. Reading Ellul was more like pulling something together that I had always known. It's different than actually learning new things. When I read *The Technological Society* I thought, well, here is a human being who's just seen the modern as it is in concrete detail around us. I'm not a great admirer of Ellul as a thinker, you see, but this *here it is, this is what it is* was wonderful for me because this is a very hard thing in the modern world to think. To get back to language again, everybody thinks they know what technology is, as if it's always been in the world, and now we just have it better; but this is not the case. So what I got from Ellul was not his theoretical understanding of what technology is, but just his recognition of its presence at every point in modern society. Wonderfully direct, immediate, practical Frenchness!

CAYLEY: What is it, in your view, that distinguishes technology from the arts and crafts which all human beings possess?

GRANT: Well, the Greek word *techne* was translated into Latin as art, and an art is simply the means of making something. What I mean by technology, and I think it's wonderfully given in the English word, is the unity of art and science. *Logos* is after all the great Greek word for science, so technology unites the word for art with the word for science. When we say the word biology, we just mean the study of life, but when, in the English-speaking world, we say technology, we're not talking about the study of art or *techne,* we are talking about something that is out there — cars, bureaucratic organizations, forms of politics, forms of economics, almost everything. It's a word that only came into English very recently, in the 1850s, I think — I may be wrong about this but I don't think you'll find the word before the 1850s. When the Germans or the French talk about what we call technology, they say technique, but I think the English word is better because it gets this unity of the arts and sciences, the unity of knowing and making, which has determined the modern world.

Knowing has been put at the service of making. In the ancient world, *techne,* or art, was a species of *poesis. Poesis* meant production, leading forth, and *techne* or art was that leading forth that depended on human beings. I call the osprey, the seahawk, which I so love, a *poesis*; it leads its own being forth in all its majesty. Now, to the ancients, art, or *techne*, was that leading forth that required human activity, like a table, a play, anything that requires that kind of leading forth by man. Technology is different from the arts, arts that always were and that people need — obviously we can't live for a minute without arts. We wouldn't have tables, we wouldn't plough the earth, etc., etc. But modern technology has something to do with will and is a summons rather than a leading forth. This relates to what I've said about objectivity. Modern technology sees everything around it as an object which is summoned forth to give its reasons.

This unity of science and art never existed in the ancient world. It is very deeply related to control; it's the unity of knowing and making, based on control. Therefore, it's something new. The idea that we've always had technology and we just do it a little better just won't go. The technologies that we have, both in penicillin and in nuclear arms, if you want to take two very different things, are things that have been summoned forth by getting things to give their reasons. The *nucleus* has been summoned forth to give its reasons, and out of that we have these amazing instruments of warfare. The things that sensible people prize about the modern come from the same source. I don't want to say that everything that has been summoned forth has not been for man's benefit. Much of it has. Think of an operation without anaesthetics; it only takes one second to be grateful for that, particularly for a man who's had all his teeth pulled.

There are a vast number of scientists who say that they just discover what the world is like and leave it up to the politicians and mankind in general to say how such discoveries should be used. This is something that is said over and over again. Now, speaking against that, Heidegger says that technology is *before* science. In other words, in modern science at its beginning, in its very origins, was this idea of control. Therefore, you can't say that Einstein's great formula $E=mc^2$ is simply telling us what the world is like and then a lot of bad people use it wrongly, because in the very formula itself is the possibility of control.

I see civilizations as dominated by particular paradigms of knowledge, which have within them the particular methods which are appropriate. One of the central paradigms of modern science is experiment, "putting nature to the question," as Bacon said. Now, one has to remember that Bacon was a lord chancellor and knew from experience what it was to put people to the question. Therefore, when he says that modern science puts nature to the question in experiment, he means this extreme control of nature which is given in the very words he uses. This is why people don't consider other forms of science which don't result in being able to control the world as real science. Heidegger argues that Aristotelian science and modern science are equally true, they're just different ways of looking at things; but most of us cannot agree because other sciences don't issue in control of the world, and we take it for granted that what makes a science true is that you're able to control the world through it.

CAYLEY: In terms of your own thinking, it seems that at the time you wrote *Philosophy in the Mass Age* you

still saw benefits of technology on one side and liabil-
ities on the other, and you thought somehow the
benefits could be "maximized," to use this terrible language, and the benefits minimized. But then, as the
1960s went on, and perhaps as you studied Heidegger
as well, you no longer saw it that way. It's not that you
then denied the benefits of technology, but that you no
longer saw it as something which we can simply use.

GRANT: This is said for the revolting reason of self-
justification, but if you live in the Western world and if
you see that what determines what the Western world
is is this paradigm of knowledge which I call technology, it is terribly difficult to put it into question
without being a fool. I've had children who've had
operations, and as I've said, I am glad they had anaes-
thetic. I probably wouldn't be alive today if certain
things hadn't been there when I was very ill, and I'm
very glad to be alive. Technology is the Western destiny and to put this into question is something one
must do in fear and trembling. The ancient world, and
many ancient worlds, depended on the terrible institution of slavery; now we have machines which liberate
people. All this must be taken into account when one
is talking about this, or else one talks nonsense, and
therefore one talks offensive nonsense. It's a question
that must be discussed with the very greatest care.

CAYLEY: But that having been said, am I right that, at
a certain point, you began to see that technology is not
simply something that we use . . .

GRANT: It is something that uses us. This takes us
back to the word *fate*. It is a Western fate, which has
now become worldwide, and it is a fate that has within
it, as even the simplest person on earth can know, the

possibility of the destruction of the human race. Only a maniac can think well of the fact that we have the possibility of ending the human race by nuclear weapons. This is the Western fate, and I think it will be lived out in the future in ways I do not know, both for good and for evil; but I also think that within it is something that cuts us off from knowledge of very important matters, which I would call knowledge of eternity, or knowledge of the beautiful.

CAYLEY: By the time you wrote some of the later essays in *Technology and Empire* you seem to have been feeling this sense of being cut off very keenly.

GRANT: Yes. It is hard to live in North America and not to see, even with all that's great about our society, that the very fabric of that society cuts us off from knowledge, which we need to have, and loves that we need to have. I'm sorry to say that about North America; but North America, I want to say first, is the only society I know. I've gone on trips to see my wife's folks in England, but I haven't really known England for forty years. I can only therefore speak of what I know, and it seems to me that in the coming to be of technological society in North America, certain things were found but many things of great importance and illumination and happiness for human beings were lost.

Some people have called me an antiquarian, but there is no point in being antiquarian because the only time any of us has to live is now. Antiquarianism is a pleasant thing for people living in a museum culture; a few people do it, there's no harm in it. But we don't really look at the past for antiquarian reasons, we look at the past to see if in looking at its thought and its art, we can see things that have been lost and that we need for this very present moment of our existing. It's for this reason only that I have stressed remembering — remembering for the sake of health now. People are so surrounded by the immediate present where things are so lost and where things are presented to them in the crazy style that results from that loss, because those doing the presenting have forgotten as much as anybody else that they need to remember. It's an extreme example, but I was watching George Will on the television — do you know this fellow? — and he suddenly said, "Of course we were the first people to have a free and democratic society." Well, one only has to think in English terms of the revolution of 1688 . . . but here he was presenting something to the Americans about their uniqueness, which is just nonsense. It does harm to every American who listens to it and takes it for granted, because they cannot judge the world in a proper way if they think this. And having imperial power, they better think as well as they can.

CAYLEY: You describe technology as a worldwide destiny, but in your essay "In Defence of North America" you also say that this is a destiny to which North America has been particularly open. Why is that?

GRANT: Clearly, its intellectual origins were in Europe, in people like Descartes. The first beginnings of what people call the industrial revolution were in England. But then why was it so magnificently incarnated in North America? I think one thing one can say here is Protestantism. A great book, for all its theoretical failings, is Weber's book *Protestantism and the Spirit of Capitalism*. It really shows you why there is something frenetic in Protestantism — to get things done and to control the world. I think it was also our pioneering origins. And so many of the pioneering Americans who controlled the United States were Protestants; pioneering people had to deal with the arts, or else they went down. I was reading the other day a book about early New Brunswick by one of my mother's relations, and they didn't kill people but they had to eat human flesh in the early days of New Brunswick. He just says it quite matter-of-factly. They'd been thrown out of the U.S., they were thrown into a very pioneering place without much support from the British government, they nearly starved to death; therefore, when people died, they had to do it. Now, I'm not saying that all pioneering society was like this, but a lot of pioneering society was mighty tough and nobody should forget that or be soft about it and not recognize the greatness.

There is the terrible side of things that were done to the Indians, but there's still something magnificent and grand about the opening of North America by pioneering Protestants, is there not? And this led people to be immensely practical. They went down unless they spent their days on practicalities. And I would say that this is another reason why people were open to a particularly controlling form of science. After all, the great theoretical scientists have largely been Europeans, though some of them came to America. But science has never been more dominating than in North American education, and you can see why it was so breathtakingly attractive to these pioneering Protestants. They incarnated it, didn't they? Detroit is, in a way, over — now it's Silicon Valley and Texas — but we lived not so very far from Detroit and it was a fabulous thought, just to think Detroit as it was when it was the dominating technological centre of America. It was an extraordinary town. I had a friend who did some advertising for General Motors in Canada, and he once went down, he was summoned down to where the board of General Motors met in Detroit, in a room much bigger than the parliament of Canada. All he had to do there was answer about a thirty-second question, but he said it was one of the unforgettable sights to see in North America.

CAYLEY: Bigger than the House of Commons?

GRANT: Bigger than the House of Commons, that's how he described it to me. This was the boardroom where people were summoned to give their reasons, to use a phrase I used about something else. Technology is not simply a matter of cars and machines and things like that; bureaucracy summons people to give their reasons as much as scientists summoned the nucleus to give its reasons.

CAYLEY: Earlier you said that technology, in its origins, has "something to do with will." What does it have to do with will?

GRANT: What happens between Mediterranean civilization, with its arts and sciences, and the civilization of the North Atlantic, England, Germany, France, Holland, etc., where technology arose is very difficult to say. At the very height of Christianity is the statement "not my will but thine," but Western Christianity has still been very concentrated on the will, the language of will is very central to Western Christianity. I'm not saying this is a sufficient explanation. Many people have tried to explain how this new science arises and comes into being with people like Galileo, and later is expressed very wonderfully by Descartes and Bacon and people like that, but I'm not sure anyone has fully grasped it.

CAYLEY: Francis Bacon says that the new science involves "putting Nature on the rack." Does the disenchantment of Nature this implies depend on Protestantism in some way?

GRANT: I would go further back and say that Christianity itself did this. If you see the world as other-than-God, which was fundamental to the doctrine of creation, then you can know it and control it in a deep way. I think Christianity is essentially responsible for the demystifying of nature, because when you look at what comes between the Greeks and modern science during the long period in which modern science was being prepared in Western Europe, what comes between is Christianity. That is just a fact.

Now, I agree with Heidegger that ancient Greek science is equally as true as modern science, but modern science is based on a very different principle: the control of human and nonhuman nature. It started out very clearly related to charity, and I think perhaps this has been the greatness of Western society, as well as its ambiguity. Western civilization has two sources: one saying the highest human act is contemplation, the other saying the highest human act is charity. Now, I'm not saying you can't put them together. In a way they are put together in modern science. But modern science is much more turned to practice, to charity, than to pure contemplation. This division between charity and contemplation is central to the Western world.

CAYLEY: In *Technology and Empire* you acknowledge that one source of technology is charity, and that controlling nature is a means to reduce suffering. But then you say that this will to good tends to turn into what you call the will to will. What did you mean by that?

GRANT: Nietzsche says the sheer will to will is what nihilism is. When there is just the desire to will, that is nihilism. Now, regarding technology, I would say that when people are simply interested in the development of technology for its own sake, it has become nihilistic. Someone who expressed this — and it's sad to speak against him because he was badly treated in the United States — was Robert Oppenheimer. I think he perfectly expressed this technological science out of control when he said, "When something is sweet, you have to go ahead with it." That means, with regard to technology, that when you can do it, you should do it. Well, surely we've seen enough of this in the Western world from many countries. This is just craziness, is it not?

I'm not a great admirer of the Kennedys, but one thing I did admire about Teddy Kennedy was his attempt to say that there should be some limitation on experiments with human life and human beings. I think this came out of his Catholicism. He lost to the scientific community — even somebody of his power — he was beaten in Congress, but I think it was a great thing to have tried to say. It's a very hard thing to say and one must be terribly careful because it could lead to all kinds of obscurantism and folly, but if we are turning away from the dear old tried-and-true method of producing human beings, I really think it would be much better to turn back from all this. When human beings no longer generate their own species, then I'm really scared. It may be primitive, but in science there is never only pure knowing, it's always related to doing and making.

There are, of course, all kinds of prudential considerations involved in deciding what we should turn back from and what not. I'm not a Catholic, and I am not saying all that is implied by some Catholics about this. I used to think it was an enormous liberation when Hegel talked about the purposes of human sexual love as being beyond procreation, and I certainly think they are beyond procreation, I think they're wonderful. But I think if human sexual love is entirely cut from generating the species — I'm not here talking about contraception — I think this will be a very gate of hell.

CAYLEY: One can obviously multiply examples of what you're talking about, but it seems particularly clear that today's so-called computer revolution is occurring without any thought as to what it means or whether it is desirable. We're having these machines because they're wonderful machines. It's a self-propelling dynamo.

GRANT: Exactly. And to stand in its way is to say that one is against the progress of knowledge, when every civilized society on earth has believed that it is good for human beings to have knowledge. Scientists use this argument to speak against those who are scared by certain things that are all around us, but I think it begs the question or, I would say, perverts the question. It's just a way of saying if anything is sweet we have to go ahead with it, and this surely is not the case.

VI
THE DECAY OF JUSTICE

CAYLEY: In 1974 you gave a series of lectures at Mount Allison University that were later published as *English-Speaking Justice*. You said a moment ago, while we were between tapes, that you gave those lectures because Alex Colville twisted your arm.

GRANT: Yes, he was an old friend. I greatly admire his painting, and I greatly admire him as a man. He was at Mount A. at this point, he hadn't yet moved to Wolfville, and he asked me to come down. Being by nature a lazy bee, it's that kind of thing that gets me to write something down.

CAYLEY: In the lectures you analysed the argument of John Rawls's then much celebrated book *A Theory of Justice*. Why did you choose that book?

GRANT: Well, you know how one begins to see new things. I think it was just an absence in me that, having grown up in the family and household that I did, I never thought that a society like Canada was based on contract. I just took it as something natural, the way that many people still do in the Maritimes. Nobody thinks they're part of Cape Breton society because of a contract. I became seriously aware of the contractarian view by accident through my belief that the graduate students I taught should know the modern. Rawls was being reviewed, so I read the book and saw it was a modern statement of contractarianism, the idea that society is all a contract between calculating individuals, and I decided that this was an extremely inadequate political philosophy. After all, Plato's greatest work, *The Republic*, is an attack on ancient contractarianism, although ancient contractarianism is not quite the same as modern contractarianism.

So I had been aware of contractarianism as a vague theory out there, but at this point it came pressingly through to me. And also my wife had led me to see that the abortion issue was very fundamental. She had led me into the right to life and into thinking about the abortion issue. A certain kind of contractarianism, individualistic contractarianism, had been expressed in the decision of the American Supreme Court in Roe v. Wade. Mr. Justice Blackmun, in this decision, says that the states of the union have no right to pass legislation about abortion, and this essentially expressed American contractarianism. After all, the American Constitution, in an intellectual sense, depended prodigiously on Locke, who was a great contractarian. I had never looked at this side of Locke before, so when

Colville wanted me to write, I wrote this book called
English-Speaking Justice, about English-speaking contractarianism.

Now, I think what's wrong with the book, completely wrong, is that I hadn't seen sufficiently deeply
the relation between contractarianism and capitalism,
that capitalism requires a certain kind of contractarianism. Contractarian theory, though it's often used by
the left, is fundamentally capitalist. I don't think it
was clear to me then how much capitalism is the most
successful modern regime; I had always thought that
this institutionalizing of greed, which capitalism is,
was something we'd get over. So I think what's wrong
with the book is that I don't relate contractarianism
sufficiently to capitalism. But I still agree with my
attack on Rawls.

CAYLEY: Let's start with Rawls then. You say that
although Rawls is a contractarian, it's a very much
vitiated contractarianism from what one would find
in Hobbes or Locke or Rousseau. What, in your view,
has the modern position been reduced to?

GRANT: I think it's a very sentimentalized view.
After all, Hobbes had said, "Continually to overpass is
felicity, continually to be overpassed is misery, to quit
the race is to die." Hobbes had a really tough view of
human existence, which Locke took over; Locke often
hid it, but he took it over. Rawls, in a sense, took it
over too, but without believing any of it. And this is
something which is so strange about the United
States. It's a very, very tough society abroad, and often
in its internal relations, as well, when it comes down
to really nitty-gritty questions like race. But in what I
would call the eastern seaboard universities there is a

sentimentalism about human beings, as if they were all rather sweet, secularized Jews or secularized Protestants. So I think a sentimentalizing of the contract theory is very deeply part of Rawls's work.

The contract theory is a tough theory. It says that the individual stands alone against the world and society is just the contract which overcomes what would otherwise be the war of each against each. Now, let's not say that there is not some truth in Hobbes and Locke. I think that people who are greater thinkers are not in contradiction with Hobbes but include what Hobbes thought within their thought. The reason so much of Plato's writing is an attempt to show the inadequacy of contractarianism is that he sees the immense partial truth in it. Hobbes is a great thinker, though Rawls doesn't mention him much. He mentions the people who talk more sweetly.

CAYLEY: He mainly mentions Kant, I think, and in your lectures you call Kant "the great delayer." Why is that?

GRANT: Well, this is Nietzsche's phrase, that Kant is the great delayer; it's one of Nietzsche's wonderful, wonderful phrases. Kant said in *The Critique of Pure Reason* that he wanted to combine an Epicurean science with a Platonic morality. Epicurus was the great ancient materialist. When the psalmist wrote "The fool has said in his heart there is no God," he might have had Epicurus in mind. What Nietzsche means about materialist science and Platonic morality is that you can't have both, can you? A lot of people in the modern world, fine people, whom we might call "liberal secularists," still want a continuation of the morality that came essentially out of Christianity, without belief.

But you can't have it, can you? Nietzsche's Zarathustra says, "The mob blinks: 'We are all equal . . . before God we are all equal . . .' But now this God has died."[119] There's no reason to believe in equality, it doesn't seem to me, unless there is some fundamental grounds for equality.

In the United States you have a constitution that was put together partly by Lockean secularists and partly by Protestants. Because it was written before the contradiction between materialist science and a morality of equality became evident, it still contains some defences for tradition. At the time we got the Charter of Rights and Freedoms in Canada I told an American friend that I preferred the British tradition in which rights are guaranteed in parliament, and he convinced me to the contrary by saying, very shrewdly, "I think that system was much better when you had people who really believed in these rights in parliament, but when you have modern people in the legislatures, it's better to have a written constitution." In a better time you don't need a written constitution but in a time like this written constitutions are a help. I think they have greatly defended things in the United States, although they have often been terribly misused. I've changed my mind on this.

CAYLEY: You say in *English-Speaking Justice* that there are a number of reasons why people haven't noticed the diminishing grounds for a belief in equality and one of them, you say, is the fact that we're such an unphilosophical people. How has this prevented us from seeing the inadequacies of contractarian theory?

GRANT: If we're talking now about Canada in particular, I think one great and good thing about Canada was that there was more innocence here, both in French- and English-speaking Canada, than in the United States or England. Don't you think that is true? And I mean innocence as quite a nice thing — I don't mean it as altogether nice, but you know, quite a nice thing. It's going now, but while it lasted these kinds of questions didn't arise for Canadians, they just took things for granted.

One thing that I think took Canadians out of their innocence at the level of political thought in Canada was Trudeau's regime. This was one of its goods. Here you had a man who was an entire contractarian, a man who certainly believed in modernity as the universal fate, a man who didn't believe in nationalism at all; and being this kind of person, he raised a lot of new questions in Canada with startling clarity, didn't he? Traditionally the Conservative Party had been the party which was filled with the more innocent of the bourgeois, those who didn't think very much, and some of them may have been led to thought. That's why I rather like them. It's one of the things I liked about Diefenbaker — he hadn't had a thought in his head. And, you know, it may be good for practical people not to have thoughts in their heads, but now we've come to the point where thoughts are necessary. That's what I mean by "innocence," and that was true in Canada.

I am certainly aware of the risk that modern technological societies, if they're not contractarian, might fall to something lower than contractarianism. People have sometimes taken national socialism in Germany as an aberration, and it certainly was in detail, but as a way of thought it was also something more universal, and that would surely be a lower form of society even than contractarian capitalism, wouldn't it? I don't understand how Western technological society could move out of contractarianism, except over many centuries. I think it could — hope is a virtue — but how it will happen I have no idea. I am sure that contractarianism is a view of human beings that cannot possibly produce decent societies. Everybody is thinking of Africa these days; I more and more wish that Europeans had never gone near the place, you know, and had let these tribal societies come to something of their own, in a real way, without this sudden importation of European contractual capitalism on top of them.

CAYLEY: The second thing which you suggest delayed recognition of the inadequacy of the contractual account of justice was the close relationship between Protestantism and liberalism. How do you understand this relationship?

GRANT: This is one of the most difficult questions to understand. I think I would put it this way: the greatest force in the Western world has been modern technological science. This was the very centre of modern liberalism, the means of changing the world to make it as we, in our freedom, wanted it. Protestantism came to be just as this science was coming to be. Its opposition in Europe was Catholicism, which stood for the older science, the science of Aristotle. Protestantism, in all its ways, was more and more breaking with the authorities of the world, the old world of landlords and clerics who had run Europe. Both modern science and Protestantism were breaking with that old world, and therefore they saw themselves as one. One sees this in a very cynical way in one of the supreme founders of modern science, Francis Bacon.

Now this is not to say that Protestantism has been only one thing. English-speaking Protestantism has been Calvinist and German Protestantism has been Lutheran, and it's interesting that out of the much greater mystical and contemplative nature of Lutheranism you get music and philosophy in Germany, while in the English-speaking world you haven't had any music, really, until the appearance of black music. I think this has to do with the influence of this very practical, down-to-earth Calvinism. People would debate this, but I think the Germans are infinitely more serious, as a philosophic people, than the English or the Americans have ever been.

Today I think you see the influence of Calvinism more within fundamentalism. The establishment Protestant churches in North America have succumbed to a vague, weak liberalism worth really nothing. Among Protestants, the fundamentalists are the people who essentially stand with Calvin. The Bible is the book, and the book is final, isn't it? They may misinterpret the book — that's another matter — but they certainly follow the great Protestant tradition that that book is central to the truth. For them that book holds in itself Jesus Christ. Now, within all religions there can be people who aren't actually sincere — that's not my business — I'm just talking about their intellectual background.

CAYLEY: How do you see Protestantism as having sustained liberalism?

GRANT: Well, Protestantism, when it was believed as Protestantism, gave liberalism a kind of moral bite, and

I suppose that in the English-speaking world this was supplied by Methodism above all. In Canada people like Mr. Woodsworth and many of the other founders of the CCF and the NDP were Methodists. They gave a kind of moral bite and moral limitation to contractualism, didn't they? Protestantism certainly wasn't saying that society was just a bare contract. It certainly wasn't saying what Kant said. Kant said you could have a perfect society made up of clever devils, because if they just were clever enough to make the contract, the society would follow. Now, Protestantism didn't really believe that. It gave the purely contractual capitalist society a moral basis.

Of the three great Western forms of biblical religion, the Protestants were the first secularized, the Jews the second, and now indeed to a very great extent the Catholics are being secularized. These religions were secularized by the contractual world they lived in — I don't mean by anything as theoretical as contractarianism, but by the contractual world they lived in — and it gradually killed them. Mainline Protestantism has become shallower and shallower and shallower in Canada, hasn't it? Catholicism has greater strength; and Judaism has the strength of being not only a religion but a race, and therefore it has this continuity that doesn't allow contractualism within its own borders, although outside it's a different matter. Now, as these religions have weakened, a more purely contractual society has arisen, and I don't think human beings will take it, will they? That's why, in *English-Speaking Justice*, I used the example of the abortion decision, because the decision was that every individual has control over their own body and that people aren't individuals until they come out of the womb, therefore you can kill the fetus at will — that's really what the decision was. Now, that is such a statement as to what human beings are. One of the powerful claims of contractualism has been that we can have a pluralist society without anybody needing to make any statements about the nature and destiny of man. But in the abortion decision you *are* making a statement about the being of the fetus you cannot escape — you're killing it, or giving the licence to kill it. In that sense the being of the world is right before you and the nature of contractarian society is exposed.

CAYLEY: You and Mrs. Grant have put a good deal of time and effort into this question of abortion. Have you engaged with the feminist view on this, and do you not think that it contains an account of justice as well, justice for women?

GRANT: Let me say just completely directly: I think the feminist cause was an excellent thing, arising in North America when it did, because women had been very badly treated, particularly in certain periods of modern North American history. I think feminists are sometimes wrong about the past, but that's a minor matter. I think the feminist cause was largely right, but I cannot see it condoning the mass slaughter of fetuses. I have been to lots of meetings where there have been lots of feminists, and I mean by "feminists," official feminists, people who are in the movement and have been leaders of the movement. I think my communication with them has always been in disagreement but in friendship. However one approaches the mass slaughter of fetuses, I think this is too deeply part of North America to use anything but persuasion and friendship in the defence of the right-to-life position. But one must remember that in *all* the polls, in *all* the polls, the highest percentage of those who desire free abortion are men between nineteen and thirty. I think the high percentage of men on that side is a fact one better remember.

For me, the whole business of abortion is related to the secular view that human beings are really just lumps of matter. I think that this view, on the part of both men and women, is much more profoundly a part of the abortion thing in the West than is feminism. What the question finally turns on is the idea that human beings are not immortal souls. The language of persons is used, but I don't see why the language of persons is good enough to speak against abortion. The language of persons says that people can *become* rational and freely choosing beings, but not that some things belong to them by nature. I think what is fundamentally at issue here is the secular thought that underlies modern North American society.

CAYLEY: One can look across a whole continuum of cases in which abortions are done and see tremendous variety. It might be little more than a convenient backstop for the careless or unlucky, or there might be extremely compelling reasons why a birth would be insupportable for a certain woman at a certain time. Can a categorical position cover this variety of cases?

GRANT: Well, there are all kinds of relativity. About the world one should be relative, in the proper sense, and absolute too. As far as rape goes, I think it has always been the case that doctors would just de facto see that an abortion took place. But, in general, I think it is clear that people are crying out for adopted chil-

dren. Another thing about which some interesting statistics have been taken — and I know the devil can
always quote statistics — is that when people look at
battered children, a large and overwhelming percentage of those battered children turn out to have been
wanted — a very strange fact, because the battering is
done above all by men. In terms of adoption, I think
Birthright is a great organization, asking women to take
the child to term and then finding proper adoption
and looking after those who are pregnant. I think this
is the central, positive side of this movement. The
woman in question may have a terrible nine months,
but the child in question is being killed and that is a
greater sacrifice. What one asks of women in holding
children to term is a large sacrifice indeed, but it is not
the sacrifice of life itself. If we say that life is a good,
which I certainly do, and that to have a human life is
a wonderful gift, for all its anguish and horrors and
tragedies, then one is saying that when one aborts one
is depriving a human being of that.

The more we can reduce suffering the better, but
large sufferings have always been asked of all kinds of
people; and to me, the loss of life *ab initio* is the greatest
suffering. Now this does not mean that I would have
one second's hesitation in saying that if a woman was
going to die or suffer serious harm she should be able
to have an abortion. Such decisions are ultimately calculations in the face of the absolute, but those kinds of
calculations are necessary for every moment of society.
Some people are sacrificed to others. One is doing this
all the time, isn't one? If I give several hours to a student one afternoon, I'm not giving it to other students;
we do this all the time in life, sacrificing some people to

others. But abortion, it seems to me, is an enormous sacrifice. And what I am fundamentally against is abortion as convenience, abortion resulting from easy calculation. I think the more prosperous people who have abortions are, the more terrible it appears.

Now let me say another thing: I take for granted that the present Pope, for whom in many ways I have great respect, made a great error in relating abortion and contraception, which I think are totally different questions — not totally different, but not the same question. On the other hand, I have some sympathy for him in what he is trying to oppose, something which is absolutely central to modernity: the emancipation of the passions. I don't mean by the passions only the sexual passions. Modern politics is taken up with the emancipation of the passion for power, capitalism is taken up with the emancipation of the passion of greed. I'm not sure that this has been a great step in human history.

CAYLEY: You have said that the abortion issue is about whether human beings are immortal souls, and you have said that the Pope made a mistake in confusing the issue of abortion with the issue of contraception. What is implied about the relation between body and soul?

GRANT: I think the question of contraception turns on whether the highest act of human love must always be open to the possibility of birth. My yes to that question is why I would say no to contraception. As for the question of the soul and the body, I think it is about as hard a question as there is. One knows, for instance, in terms of the biblical religions, that Islam and Judaism and Christianity all have different answers. Hinduism, for reasons I don't altogether understand, strictly prohibits abortion, even though it's not an essentially theistic religion. I'm not saying it's atheistic or that it's polytheistic, I'm saying it is not essentially theistic. I really think this question is very hard to speak about, although the French scientist who spoke in front of the Senate committee on this when Reagan was first in power — I've forgotten his name — was very good. He just made it very clear scientifically how soon the uniqueness of the fertilized embryo is there — almost from the moment of conception. So this lucid French scientist, who appeared at great length before the Senate committee in the United States, made this uniqueness very clear. Now, as a modern scientist, he was speaking simply of the forms of life, he wasn't speaking of the idea of soul. Souls were removed from nature at the time of Descartes, weren't they? The idea of soul was that the soul of the tree was what made a tree a tree; the soul of the cow was what made a cow a cow. There was vegetative soul and animal soul and rational soul, as far as the world went, and indeed people believed that the world as a whole had a soul, didn't they? Now, this whole way of thinking that was so deeply part of the ancient world is quite gone, and if one is going to enter a public controversy, one cannot use that kind of language. It would be absurd.

However, it is the disappearance of the idea of soul from all thought in the West which has led to the massiveness of abortion. Of course, it's also led to the massiveness of population in the West, which confuses the question, doesn't it? I mean, one has to remember that France was a country of forty million and England of seven million and then a few years later England was forty-five million and France was still forty. The technological revolution has affected everything everywhere, hasn't it? And, in the face of these difficulties, it's very hard to think. I find it particularly difficult when an intensely matriarchal society, like Hinduism, is being asked by the West to slaughter its children in the name of the good of the West. I think that is wild. A very great and learned Hindu once said to me, after I had told him that my wife was very busy with something, "The only thing greater than God is the mother." Now, this was a highly philosophic, intelligent man — far more intelligent than I am — and I just thought that was so interesting. It tells you something, doesn't it?

CAYLEY: Is your opposition to easy abortion part of some larger moral concern?

GRANT: Well, I think that everybody on earth should have moral concern as much as they can. One has moral concern in those one teaches, but one doesn't teach the people for whom we ought to have the greatest moral concern: the weak of society. This is why I have feelings about the mentally retarded, and people like that, as well as about the fetus. It's the weak for whom I fear in advanced technological society. There's a way in which our society cares about the weak but there's a way in which technological society very much does not care about the weak. I think there's no getting away from what Christ said: "I was hungry and you gave me no meat; I was thirsty and you gave me no drink; I was a stranger, and you took me not in; naked, and you clothed me not; sick and in prison, and you visited me not" (Matthew 25:42–43).

Therefore, I don't want to press my moral concern because I turned away to think and to teach, which is a very different thing from the greatest moral concerns. That I am clear about. These are alternatives. Both are necessary.

CAYLEY: In *English-Speaking Justice* you express the fear that easy abortion is a harbinger which presages a time in which the weak will not retain their rights. You say that this is because a contract theory of justice is inadequate to protect those rights. But it seems to me that in some way there is greater concern in our world about those rights than ever before. Do you not agree?

GRANT: This may be off the point, but something really struck me during Watergate. I agree of course that one can't have the president of the United States breaking the law and he had to go, but the ways he'd broken it had been pretty minor, and this insistence on right inside the boundaries of the United States while this massive bombing of Cambodia and Vietnam was going on, and considering what the United States has done elsewhere in the world, suggested to me an extraordinarily divided mind. I think that one shouldn't get on too far about rights in an imperial society because they are different at home than abroad, very much so.

Now, I think it is true that things go up and down. I have a son who works with the retarded. Their situation in terms of getting out into society seems to be in some ways improving, in other ways they are more and more being pushed away and aside. Abortion is an issue for the retarded. And then there is the whole question of euthanasia among the aged, and now euthanasia among the young. There's a massive program of euthanasia going on among the young.[120]

I don't want to utter easy platitudes about such a complex thing, but I find this extremely worrying.

CAYLEY: Perhaps it's the case that where people can speak for themselves institutionalized rights are being strengthened, but at the same time obligations are weakening.

GRANT: I think they are. And that makes me fear for the rights of those people who cannot speak for themselves, the unborn and the just born, the old, and the poor.

VII
THE MULTIVERSITY

CAYLEY: I would like to talk now about the university curriculum and your career as a university teacher. You've written about the way the university curriculum has fragmented during your time, and I'm wondering if we can establish some sort of historical benchmark against which to understand these changes by going back to your grandfather's time. He was the principal of Queen's University in the late nineteenth century. What would the university have been like in his day?

GRANT: Well, when you talk about my grandfather, he was one of these secularized Protestants. I don't think he entirely admitted he was, but he was one of the supreme believers in progress and he took over a curriculum that would have been taken for granted.

Ontario at that stage was just out of the pioneering era. An artist said to me the other day about a painting he'd done of Grandfather Grant out in the country that he'd painted it because his granddad had told him that he used to set aside a dozen eggs a week to give to Queen's, and this was a big sacrifice to this fellow's granddad. Therefore, we're talking about a society where there wasn't much money to go around. It would probably be better to talk about the curriculum in a less simple society than Canada was in the 1870s. The United States had already had a settled society on the eastern seaboard for a much longer time. The question is complex for Canada because it was to a great extent a question of just keeping the traditional arts and sciences going as best they could, and they thought they'd done damn well to keep them going at all because they had so little money.

CAYLEY: I didn't mean to paint Queen's as Oxford or anything, but just to get an idea of a time at which people still thought they knew what a proper education was, and to establish a contrast with the contemporary multiversity, as you've called it.

GRANT: They took for granted that people should learn the languages of their society and, beyond that, the languages of the ancient world, and that these languages and mathematics formed the basis for going into the professions. For those who didn't go into the professions and were going to become more thoughtful, these people would go on to philosophy and through philosophy some of them would go on to theology. They mostly believed that they ought to have some philosophy before they did the theology. So languages and mathematics with some physics and chemistry constituted a general education and from there they would go on to professional education. Somebody once said in a Canadian university — I forget who it was — in the nineteenth century: "This will do you good and help your emoluments." I think they thought these together. You had to have this general linguistic education to be able to do anything in law. Medicine would still have been incomparably less scientific — you had to know some chemistry and some biology, and then you left the university to do anatomy. I think this was the general idea of the education.

Now, the multiversity is such a new thing, isn't it? Technological society requires an enormous number of highly specialized people, and the multiversity is to a very great extent a product of that, is it not? It produces all kinds of specialists to serve the technological society. Now, some people in the university want more than that, particularly certain theoretical scientists, who know, despite all I have said about the unity of making and knowing in modern science, that the highest science is still deeply theoretical. I mean by theory knowing for knowing's sake. Therefore, this has continued. The people whom I have admired most in Canadian universities are the purely theoretical scientists, and because they are at the same time necessary, extremely necessary to the technological society, they have been able to keep some good things in the way of studies for their own sake. Theoretical scientists are the people who have often helped me most greatly, because they know there is something to be known, and they know how difficult it is to know it, how sheerly difficult it is to know physics. I don't want to go back on what I've said elsewhere. There is something in modern physics, as I said about $E = mc^2$, that leads immediately to being able to do things, but natural science still has its theoretical basis. Let me put it this way: Theory remains in the universities more in certain natural sciences than anywhere else. It isn't as demolished as in the social sciences or in what is called philosophy or indeed in literature. Literature is often taught quite nicely — junior colleagues go out and teach nice things to young people — but studies of literature are more and more technological, are they not?

CAYLEY: How do you mean "technological" in the context of the study of literature?

GRANT: Well, let me see if I can put this clearly. I mean, there are great industries in the analysis of literature and the history of literature, which seem to me to take one quite far, often, from the beauty of literature.

CAYLEY: Over the period in which you have taught in Canadian universities, from 1947 until 1984, you must have witnessed a remarkable transformation, at least according to how I imagine Dalhousie in 1947.

GRANT: Yes, one of the nice things about being at Dalhousie in '47 was that that transformation hadn't yet happened. Transformations that are necessary to the technological apparatus sometimes happen more slowly in Nova Scotia. Watching what happened to places like the University of British Columbia and then to the State University of New York when I moved to McMaster impressed me very much. There was much to be said for these changes democratically; but the State University of New York got more every year than the whole endowment of Harvard, the richest university in the world. That gives you a picture. The University of Toronto was rather different because it had some history from before the age of progress and its college system mediated the directness of the changes that happened elsewhere. Those universities in Ontario which had some history generally did better than those which didn't because they had something to carry over, and this was true of McMaster because it retained remnants of the Baptist tradition from which it had come. But as one watched — and this is just my experience, I only know what I saw — McMaster was more and more turned in the direction of extremely technological research. It was better in this way than many others because the social sciences weren't as strong at McMaster, and the worst abuses of the modern university, it seems to me, have happened in the social sciences. There was less abuse in the natural sciences because they are authentically what this tradition came from and therefore they are less easily corrupted. These people are all necessary to the state and therefore they have great influence in this society.

But let me here admit my own utter failure. I tried at McMaster to build a department of religion in which people who were inside the great religions of the world expounded the truth of those religions — that's what I was going to do. Now, through mistakes I made, it gradually got taken over by people who just did research about the great religions. You know, you can write endless books about the Bible without caring an iota whether what you've written has anything to do with the truth that is given in the Bible; you can write endless books about old Sanskrit texts without knowing anything about the truth of the Vedanta — do you see? And this is a progressively building thing. Young professors know that they get their promotions and their tenure by doing research, which is the very core of the university. Now, I think there are both pragmatic and theoretical reasons for doing research. Research can be useful, but because it so dominates the university, it takes over those things that need to be known but which cannot be known by research. It takes over functions of the university which cannot be fulfilled by researching. If young people in universities know that they will build their careers in certain ways, then some people will resist, but not many. We all know that there are certain requirements, given in the ends of corporations, which we have to follow if we are going to get anywhere in those corporations. Well, that's equally true of universities.

CAYLEY: You said a moment ago that the social sciences are the most corrupted, that because natural science is, in effect, the paradigm of knowledge itself, it is the humanities that are most corrupted because they adopt methods not proper to them. Is that more or less what you're saying?

GRANT: They call themselves "social sciences," don't they? Mathematizable research has been very deep in the social sciences and mathematizable research is farther away from what is being studied in the social sciences than it is from what is being studied in physics or chemistry. I mean, mathematizable research can tell you a lot about the planets; it may not be able to tell you the final truth about the planets, but it can tell you a lot, and it can get you out there, indeed. But, in the social sciences, mathematizable research has been so pervasive that those people who haven't fallen into it have often fallen into some other kind of mumbo-jumbo. Now, this is also true of the humanities, but there at least there is a given corpus. I mean, if your business is to expound Shakespeare, then whatever you do, there before you is the supreme genius and therefore it's harder to be corrupted than if what is before you is a sociological analysis of the city of Toronto.

CAYLEY: Have you already, in effect, stated the reason you resigned from McMaster in saying what happened in your department?

GRANT: Yes. I thought research had taken over the proper purposes of the department of religion and that I had indeed failed to build a department of religion in which I could live. People who are enormous experts are necessary — people, let's say, who are enormous experts in what has been done in the last hundred years in the study of the Bible, or in the philological study of Sanskrit — such people are necessary, but the point is to know the truth of the Vedanta, the truth of the gospels. The means has become the end. In biblical research, they've gone over the Bible word for word, and I'm not terribly sorry about that, but it has happened at a time when the truth of the Bible has become less and less important to people, and I think there is some connection between the two. The case is certainly the same in the study of Indian religion. I think it's great to have people around, in the same way you would have waitresses around, to know about the philology in Sanskrit, but the point is to try and see what is true about the Vedanta.

CAYLEY: When you say that you failed, I wonder how you mean it, because it seems to me you've tried to demonstrate that this is the overwhelming tendency . . .

GRANT: . . . of the modern world.

CAYLEY: Could you have succeeded?

GRANT: You know, as always, one fails through laziness and lack of attention. There's not only the failing against the spirit of the age, which I think was given, but there are also all the failures that arise from one's own silly vices — you know, laziness, etc., etc. But indeed it may have been that the kind of thing I wanted in the university was impossible. I'm very grateful to McMaster. When I went there I had just had the trouble of resigning from York, and I loved some of the theoretical scientists at McMaster, they're splendid and wonderful people. But gradually the spirit of this technical, modern research, which is just part of technology, took over what I had been trying to do in the department of religion. How does one know what is inevitable and what is not? One never does know. Could one have done better? These kinds of questions one just doesn't know about in life, does one?

CAYLEY: You resigned shortly before you would have retired.

GRANT: Five years before, yes.

CAYLEY: Did you hope to achieve something by your resignation?

GRANT: It was economically costly to me, and as a Scotsman I care about economics, naturally, because I've had six children. I was hoping I was saying no to what had become the dominant spirit in what I would call the arts faculties at the universities. Obviously the spirit of modern science is going to be triumphant in the parts of the universities that are concerned with that, but I was hoping I could say no to this spirit's entry into the arts faculties at the universities. I don't know whether I did or not — how does one ever know anything of that kind?

CAYLEY: But you did it at cost to yourself.

GRANT: Yes, but I don't want to make it sound as if I did it on a great matter of principle. I did resign from York on a big matter of principle, years before, but in the case of McMaster, I just couldn't be bothered to spend the last five years of my working life in this arts faculty, and particularly in this department of religion, which I thought had just become a home for the stupidest kind of technology. It was in a way an act of impatience, which may be good or bad, I don't know. I don't want to build it up in any way; it was just an act of impatience with what the arts faculty had become at McMaster.

CAYLEY: As a teacher, you haven't been confined by the university. You've been a public person, and you've been widely read and consulted on the questions of the day. Yet some critics have said of your teaching that, in the end, you can't offer a positive politics or say what people ought to do.

GRANT: Well, I think first of all that whatever the relation between the theoretical and the practical life there is bound to be some division, and so there is something nonsensical about giving immediate advice to people who have to carry it out practically. I think there is something impudent about that. I mean, one of the silly consequences of democracy has been the idea that everybody should be interfering in every moment of government in a way that just makes any ordered society impossible. That would be the first thing I would say. Secondly, I would say that anybody who carries theories so far that he says that it doesn't matter what happens is just an ass. What everybody does finally matters — whether they are theoretical or practical people.

Anybody who has time to think has been given a great privilege by society. Most people are very much confused, particularly in a world this extremely complex, and with the journalistic media in the United States banging away to teach them that the world is a certain way. Though many people may be aware of the darkness of modernity, they don't know what it is, and therefore I think it is very important to try and say what the present is as clearly as one can, because it isn't as if it were obvious what the present is. You know, this week it's Reagan's colon, next week . . . etc., etc. Even if people are simply passive recipients of news, they still have to live and they have to try to understand the society as they meet it. There is a great advantage to people in beginning to understand things rather than meeting the world as just un-understandable chaos, even though much of what we have to meet is un-understandable chaos.

CAYLEY: I know you'll laugh if I say there is any affinity between your thought and John of the Cross, but it seems to me that the idea of the dark night of the soul is germane to some of your writings. Instead of adopting the language of problems and solutions, you've written about "bringing the darkness into light as darkness," which seems to me to say, in effect, that the only way out is through, that the only way we can find the light is by experiencing the darkness and deprivation in which we live.

GRANT: The distinction between mysteries and problems has always meant a lot to me. After all, there is such a thing as a problem to which there is a solution, but mysteries are things one lives in the presence of. For instance, the mystery on which Simone Weil dwells of the perfection of God and the misery of man — that's not a problem, that's a mystery. And one must remember when one talks of problems and solutions that some people once talked of the "final solution" of a particular problem, which meant the concentration camps. There are obviously problems and solutions, but one better be careful of the words with such an example before us.

Now, having said that, what I mean by "mysteries" are those great questions without solution that will always exist for human beings wherever they are, and these are what I have been above all interested in thinking about. It's been very much the American way to, as we say, "face" problems, which means settle them and get on with running things. But there are some questions which I would call mysteries, and one of the great purposes of life is to spend one's life trying to enter more and more deeply into them.

I think that's what philosophy is. This is why people say, where does philosophy get you? It gets you into these great mysteries, which are endless. By entering into them one knows in some ways less, in some ways more. Darkness consists above all in cutting these mysteries out of our lives altogether. I have been trying, in talking about darkness, to hold the mysteries before people. These questions have existed in Hinduism and Buddhism as much as in Christianity. I'm not saying it's a particularly Christian thing. Darkness also hides problems, and it's very important to say what are the real problems. But I think it is bad to look at the world as altogether problems.

VIII
THE EAGLE AND THE DOVE

CAYLEY: Can we speak now about Simone Weil and about what her importance has been for you?

GRANT: Let me start by saying that we're here in the presence of a being who is quite different from those people we've talked about as great thinkers alone. I have no doubt at all that she is, in the traditional categories of the West, a great saint, and you know, many very splendid thinkers aren't remarkably saintly people, in one way or another. With Simone Weil you have to combine this staggeringly clear intellect with something that is quite beyond the intellect, namely sanctity. And I mean by saint those beings who give themselves away.

Now, there's a low order of giving oneself away

which you see in people who are absolutely occupied by a particular vice and have in that sense given themselves away; but I mean giving themselves away in love. Simone Weil to me is the supreme teacher of the relation of love and intelligence, and one must be very hesitant about somebody like this. What is it for a person like myself to look at somebody who exists not just at the level of intelligence but at the level of something which is clearly more important, as far as I am concerned — the divine love and that love in human beings. How can I say what I have learned from her? Here one lives a fairly ordinary life, doing one's best, making mistakes, full of vices, etc., and here's somebody who, in some absolutely majestic way, has passed beyond all that. When one faces a being like Francis of Assisi, or Christ, one passes right outside the great interest in the history of philosophy and things like that. I mean, St. Francis — and I take this as a fact — received the stigmata, he received on his body the wounds of Christ because of his love of the afflicted and the poor. Now, I feel that with Simone Weil I'm talking of a being like that, and this is therefore extremely hard. I just wanted to say that first.

CAYLEY: You've described her as both an intellectual and saint. Is there a tension between her sanctity and the importance she attaches to philosophy?

GRANT: Well, there have been intelligent saints. You can't be much smarter than St. John of the Cross, who was kept by the church in a ghastly cell where he could neither stand up nor sit. And yet, if one reads *The Ascent of Mount Carmel*, it's extremely intelligent. Certainly Francis is extremely intelligent, but it is true that, in his case, he attacks philosophy outright; he says, you should just be lovingly afflicted, because philosophy takes time. St. John of the Cross is nearer to Simone Weil. There isn't the same conflict in the Indian tradition. There's a wonderful, serene tranquillity about India in many ways, with all the hunger and wars and things. The greatest tradition of Hinduism has a magnificent, serene tranquillity. I don't mean by this anything like complacency, I just mean that in the West there is a greater tension than there is in the East.

In any event, Simone Weil certainly combines high intelligence with the supremacy of charity. *Charity* has become such a lousy word, I just like to use *love*; for human beings, charity is just loving what is other than yourself, so I use that word for that reason. Simone Weil came from an outstanding intellectual tradition. You know how tight the French intellectual tradition is, and she graduated with much higher marks than Sartre and Simone de Beauvoir. Someone said to me about her brother André that what Einstein is to physics he is to modern mathematics. So she was surrounded by people who combined the wonderfully sharp, clear, French interest in the intellect and the Jewish interest in the intellect, because her family were by tradition Jewish, though not believing Jews. Do you remember what Crashaw said about St. Theresa: "For all the eagle in her, all the dove." Simone Weil is the eagle and the dove, this wonderful, formidable power of intellect, with this life of giving herself away to the afflicted of the world.

CAYLEY: One of the questions on which you have acknowledged a debt to Simone Weil is the relationship between necessity and the good. Could you speak about that?

GRANT: Yes, well, this she takes from a famous quotation of Plato's in *The Republic*, in which he says that there is an infinite distance which separates the order of necessity from the order of good, and from this quotation so much of her thought comes. One means by "necessity" simply that if I tripped, I would fall. Necessity is like gravity, as she says, it's something that we are all part of: we are all going to die; if you eat too much, like myself, you get fat, etc. And this order of necessity exists also in human things, where we now think our freedom is greater. In politics, there are certain necessities. A lot of people who think about politics think there aren't, but there are necessities; people are moved by class interests, people are moved by sexual interests, etc. In all realms, there's necessity.

The order of the good enters the human world when human beings are moved by their love of perfection. There have been in our tradition arguments for the being of God, and Weil's argument, if you want to use that word, is always the argument from perfection, or as it has been called in the tradition, "the ontological argument," namely that it is clear that human beings cannot get better by their own efforts, they can only get better insofar as they have partaken in an idea of perfection. To her that is an argument for God's being. And as in Plato, the word *good*, in its completeness, would be for her an identical word with God, would it not? It just means the same thing. She says about love, and this is an extreme statement but there is something to it: "A village idiot who loves the good knows more than Aristotle."

Necessity is for Simone Weil that order which God must cross to love God. I don't like at all language about God which uses personal pronouns, but you don't improve on those who say "God himself" or "God herself" by saying "God itself." Therefore, I have a difficulty; I just want to say "God," and if God is love, then God clearly is not, as I've said, a simple unity. God is love means that God is love! It means God is loving right now. For love to be perfect to Simone Weil it has to cross an infinite distance; the highest love is that love which crosses an infinite distance. This is what the crucifixion means to her: on the cross Christ expresses his love for his enemies, he expresses his desolation, the cry of dereliction in which he feels cut off from God's transcendence, and yet he crosses that infinite distance. Simone Weil is very much like that tradition which has been central in parts of Christianity. She is essentially a theologian of the cross.

The infinite distance between God and God is necessity. The necessity which God has to cross to love God is the cross. That's what she is saying. It is impossible to think of God as a simple unity if you say that God is love, because love is always a relation.[121]

CAYLEY: Where, by way of contrast, would God be conceived as a simple unity?

GRANT: I think this is what made her leave Judaism. She felt in Judaism that God was thought of too much as a simple unity, as indeed would be the case in Islam too. This is Christianity's criticism of Judaism and Islam, and I want to say it in the gentlest fashion. It explains why Christianity seems in a certain way closer to Hinduism than it does to its fellow religions that arose in the Middle East.

CAYLEY: Can you say more about how Simone Weil conceives of God's relationship to the world?

GRANT: Simone Weil is the being who expresses most deeply, as far as I'm concerned, the moment of God's absence from the world. In Christian theology there have been two traditions: the positive tradition and the negative tradition. The positive tradition moves to God through the world; the negative tradition moves to God by negating the world. The negative tradition is in its essence Platonism, and the positive tradition is in its essence Aristotelianism, and certainly Simone Weil is on the side of the negative tradition. The negative tradition is expressed, it seems to me, in her statement, "I am ceaselessly torn by the perfection of God and the misery of human beings." The fact that we see here below the affliction of human beings has always been the deepest traditional argument against God's being. How can you look at this world and say it comes forth from love? It seems to me that almost anybody who has thought at all must have thought of this very early, and Simone Weil was brought up in this extreme and very noble French secularism.

Coming to belief in God was for her an entire surprise. Her parents, who loved her very dearly, did not know at the time she died that she believed in God, because when she wrote to her parents she did not use the word *Christ*. They were very loving, wonderful people, but she thought because they were traditionally Jewish it might offend them, or at least surprise them, so she always used instead the word *Krishna*, the great incarnate God of India.

It is a staggering event which one hardly dares talk about, but she says Christ came down to her as immediately as you and I are sitting here. And I believe this happened; I just think it happened. These things happen very occasionally and are very strange and what are we to say about them? She had been in the Spanish Civil War, she had worked in a motor factory and experienced the extreme unpleasantness of French proletarian life in the 1930s and how the wealthy French exploited the poor. And she says Christ came to her just as immediately as you and I are here in this room.

This was three or four years before she died, and it was in terms of this that she turned to look at philosophy as it was given by Plato. You see, in the kind of high French mathematical and philosophic education that she had, she must have learned Descartes and Kant and the modern philosophers just backwards to do as well as she did. But now she wanted to understand what Plato means by the idea of good — that is God, or ultimate purpose — to take it seriously in a way that modern philosophy had never taken it seriously, and to try to understand the affliction of the world in terms of an acceptance of this perfection. She says often that when you contemplate God, you should have in your mind the seventy thousand slaves that Crassus crucified when he put down the slave rebellion in Rome as a symbol of the appalling affliction that has occupied human life.

CAYLEY: I'm not sure just what it is in Plato that helps Weil, or is necessary for her understanding of her experience of Christ.

GRANT: Well, Plato is the philosopher who says very clearly that the intelligence is enlightened by love. If you take so much of the modern way of looking at things, one says that one knows things by holding them apart from oneself as objects, that love really darkens the intellect. If we're going to be objective about people, we shouldn't love them. And there's some truth in this in the law, for example. Judges should disqualify themselves from decisions regarding their own children. This is perfectly clear. And it is perfectly clear what the objective spirit has achieved in modern science. But for some things you only know them as you love them. This is my fundamental criticism of the contractual view of justice, that justice is a contract between human beings that they have calculated. But if that is so, why should people love justice? People come to know justice by loving it, don't they? This is presumably what the saints are: people who have done, probably early on, some acts of justice, and then, in the light of these acts, have seen more and more about human beings and gone on to higher and higher acts of justice.

I don't like at all the Western language that holds apart love and justice. You know how people talk this way. It's a bad form of talking. I would say the crucifixion is a supreme act of justice on Christ's part — not that he was crucified but that he submits to crucifixion. It's a supreme act of justice to love his enemies. I just don't like the view in the Western world that justice is something elementary and then there is love beyond it, because I don't see, on that view, how there could be any justice. One sees this very clearly in the fact that when people saw other races as non-people — that is, they had no love for them — then they could not be just!

CAYLEY: I'm still worrying this question about what it was that Simone Weil took from the ancient Greeks that completed or complemented what she took from Christianity.

GRANT: Let me say two things: First, if you have an immediate experience of the perfection of God, you then have to think it, do you not? Simone Weil was a perfectly practical person; she had run unions, she had worked as a school teacher, she had fought in Spain, and all this had to be thought in relation to this immense experience. She found that what is given in Plato allowed her to think the two together.

The second thing I would say is that she had seen in some very deep way that there was something wrong with the modern experiment, both practically and theoretically. She knew the great modern thinkers, as I have said. She knew Descartes and Kant in detail. She had lived with the writings of Marx. She was a friend of Trotsky, a great friend of Trotsky. Trotsky always called her *"la vierge rouge,"* and they had a very comic and amusing friendship. Her family protected Trotsky and his guards in their own house at the time when assassins from Russia were after him. Now, knowing all this about the modern, she still said a fundamental "no" to modern thought and to much of modern practice. So when she came to this great experience, where was she to find some means of thinking this experience and thinking what she was thinking about modernity, unless she turned to something before modernity, and of course Plato is the supreme before-modernity.

CAYLEY: What was the basis of her rejection of the modern?

GRANT: It's not easy to say, because remember that Simone Weil — and this is the great difficulty about reading her — was immensely busy all her life. During the last years of her life, after her experience of Christ, the war was going on. Her parents *had* to be got out of France when the Germans approached because they were Jewish, and they would have been killed. So she got them over to America and then came back and tried to get DeGaulle to drop her into occupied France. Therefore, most of her writings are in notebooks. She had been trained by her teacher, if she had half an hour in the day, to always write something down to get her head clear, and consequently, nearly all her thinking is in these small extracts from notebooks. One of the things she wrote that I think is central is quite a short piece, called "The Pythagorean Doctrine," in which she takes Pythagoras as the foundation of Platonism. Her mother told me that she wrote it in two days during their escape from France.[122] These Jews were kept in a hot, hot waiting place in Tunisia, a great big hall where they were all just packed in. Dr. and Mrs. Weil were against a wall; so was Simone. They had nothing to do, so she sat down and wrote "The Pythagorean Doctrine." It is just out-of-this-world. I mean, can you imagine — the bathrooms, the water, etc. They had escaped from France but were still in de facto occupied territory in a crazy place. She wrote things under these conditions.

The only writing of hers intended as a book, and even it is not completed, was done in London, just at the end of her life. She was working for DeGaulle, and he asked her to write a piece about what France should be like after its occupation by the Germans was over. She wrote in a very penetrating way about changes in schooling. Of course, DeGaulle thought she was a maniac. He had been thinking of how to organize municipal government and things of that kind. But one thing about the French tradition you have to realize is that quite apart from economic class, there are these people who have gone to the *grandes écoles*, the great schools of central France, and they all know one another. DeGaulle would have known about Simone Weil from way back because she had been a very great star of these *écoles*. But when he read what she had written, he could not see that it had anything to do with any future that this very practically minded, political general could possibly think about.

CAYLEY: So you're saying there's no simple way to answer the question what was the basis of her rejection of the modern?

GRANT: No, because it just seems to take place. There was a period just before she had to get her parents out, when she had a little spare time to write, and the manuscripts she produced at that time are just a changeover from her earlier writings. She's always writing about about what she calls "*la source grecque*" and the Pythagorean doctrine, and therefore, it is clear by implication that she has found Descartes and Kant inadequate, but she never says it.

CAYLEY: There's a striking section in *The Need for Roots* where she says that what is fundamentally at fault in the development of materialistic science is an incorrect notion of providence.[123]

GRANT: I've never thought of it in this language, so say more.

CAYLEY: Well, I think she's saying that the notion of a personal God who providentially and selectively interferes in human affairs creates a split between science and religion. It collapses "the infinite distance which separates the order of necessity from the order of good" and forces science to separate itself from religion, because science, to be science, must insist that the reality it studies is pure necessity and not subject to this kind of capricious intervention. She quotes, in support of her view, the passage in the Gospel of Matthew in which it is said that God "makes his sun to rise on the evil and the good, and sends rain on the just and on the unjust."[124] Weil seems to me to be saying, in other words, that true science and true religion are quite compatible. The trouble comes when religion is corrupted and science reacts by banishing the idea of the good altogether. Is that how you understand her?

GRANT: I think this is exactly what she's saying, but before I address it, let me first make another proviso. I understand neither ancient mathematics nor modern mathematics, so I have little right to speak about either. Indeed I wrote to her brother, who, as I said, is a very great mathematician, and just asked, "Is what she is saying about Greek mathematics and modern science adequate?" He wrote back that she had gotten one detail wrong about quantum mechanics, but he added that in general her writings on mathematics are to be taken with the greatest seriousness. Now, this is a person who would not say this if he did not think it.

I think what you have said is very well put. The division between science and other forms of knowledge is just folly itself, and the separation of science from the idea of the good is certainly the cause of this disunity. But as I said, I am extremely hesitant to speak about this because of my lack of knowledge of mathematics. That's why I wrote to her brother — because I wanted to know, and he did know.

There's a connection here also with Leo Strauss. Strauss had a friend named Klein, who was a student of Heidegger's, and he came out here and wrote an out-standing book called *Greek Mathematics and the Spirit of Algebra*. The Greeks didn't have algebra; algebra and calculus are the great modern forms of mathematics. Now, I have had students who do know some mathematics read this and explain it to me, but I do not feel confident in talking about it. To understand the difference between modern algebra and Greek geometry and the steps that were taken whereby all mathematics was turned into algebra in the modern world would have required of me a lifetime of study, and I have been thinking about other things. I don't want to appear to know things I don't know.

CAYLEY: Of course. In this same section of *The Need for Roots* to which I just referred, Weil says, "The true definition of science is this: the study of the beauty of the world." Has this idea of the beautiful in her thought been important for you?

GRANT: Yes, this is something that I have come to think about more and more. I realized when I was trying to think what love was that we only love what appears to us beautiful. What was so miraculous about St. Francis was that he could find beautiful things that we don't generally find beautiful. And this was also the thing that came to me as such an enormous surprise about Simone Weil: the absolute centrality for her thought of the doctrine of the beauty of the world. This was somebody who had seen war, so how can one then think the beauty of the world?

I've been thinking very hard about this, and one thing that has become clear to me is that the paradigm of knowledge given in modern science excludes from its origins the idea that one is given knowledge through love of the beautiful. I see this. I see it, for instance, in Bacon. Bacon, one of the great founders of modern science, says that poetry is just the way we speak when we are trying to convince ourselves the world is pretty when it's not really pretty. Bacon just says this directly in *The Advancement of Learning*, and it's no wonder that this has had such a terrible effect — why art has done so badly in the modern world. In the original Greek, poetry is just the word for making; it is strangely translated in the modern word production as "leading forth." Anything that any human being leads forth in a great work of art is *poesis*, it's poetry. Poetry was supposed to teach people things, teach them the truth about things. And cutting this off, cutting the beautiful off from science, except as an experience of the scientist, has I think had a very terrible effect on the way we look at the world.

CAYLEY: "Cutting it off except as an experience of the scientist" — you mean that the scientist takes his experience of beauty for a purely subjective feeling?

GRANT: Yes. Scientists say, if they have a formula whereby they can understand the world, that they find the formula beautiful, but they aren't finding the world beautiful. If you take *The Origin of Species*, it isn't telling you the world is beautiful, is it? It is certainly telling one something that is true, but beauty is somehow detached from truth in modernity, isn't it? You don't find this cutting off of the beautiful from the true in Plato's *Symposium* or *Phaedras*. Everybody is interested in art now, but what they expect to learn from it has nothing very much to do with truth. Art has more and more become entertainment, which it clearly is not with Mozart. It entertains; Mozart knew as well as anybody you had to entertain people, and he damn well did, in a marvellous way, but that's quite different from saying that art finally is entertainment. I remember when the head of the Ontario Arts Council said to me that *Figaro* was just the *South Pacific* of its age, and I knew the Ontario Arts Council would never get to first base. *South Pacific* was an early musical comedy with Mary Martin, and it's quite an amusing musical comedy, but it is not the greatest comedy ever written, which is *Figaro*, and which teaches one endlessly about the relation of beauty and truth.

CAYLEY: Let me ask a final question about Simone Weil. Her idea of necessity, understood both as beauty and affliction, is something you would have been familiar with from when you first read *Waiting for God* in the early 1950s. Later you read Strauss, and one of the great points Strauss makes is that technology as the overcoming of chance is, in a sense, the overcoming of necessity. Did you in some way connect these two thinkers?

GRANT: Well, I have partaken of these thinkers only partially, but of course all questions are one because truth is one. To deny that God is a simple unity is not to deny that God is a unity and that God is truth. One comes at questions from different directions depending on the accidental and unimportant facts of one's own life, but that does not mean that one does not have to try and think them together.

Now, I am trying at the moment to write down something based on Simone Weil's saying that faith is the experience that the intelligence is enlightened by love. I'm trying to think what this means. It is clear that modern science, or what I would call modern technological science, has not believed that the intelligence is directly illuminated by love. The scientist can love doing what he's doing, he can love wanting to know what the nucleus is, but she is saying something beyond that, that only in loving something do you know what it is. Therefore, I am trying to write something about how the knowledge that the intelligence is enlightened by love has been put aside in our multiversities, and about how it can be reclaimed as knowledge. That's what all my thoughts are turned on now. Having learned a great deal from Strauss and Heidegger and people like that, I am now almost entirely thinking about what Simone Weil thinks about. I hate to say "thinking positively," because so many B.S.ers in the United States talk that way — asses talk about thinking positively — but I want to think less about what is wrong with the modern and more about the truth of what is not present in the modern.

NOTES

1. Grant was also featured in the final program of an earlier series of mine called "Richard Cartwright and the Roots of Canadian Conservatism" (CBC Radio, 1984, transcript available). The discussion, which also featured Northop Frye and S. F. Wise, concerned the fate of loyalism and the interpretation of Canadian history.

2. William Christian, *George Grant: A Biography* (Toronto: University of Toronto Press, 1993), 348.

3. Charles Taylor, *Radical Tories: The Conservative Tradition in Canada* (Toronto: House of Anansi Press, 1982), 129.

4. Christian, *George Grant*, 112.

5. Louis Greenspan, "George Grant Remembered," *Two Theological Languages by George Grant and Other Essays in Honour of His Work,* ed. Wayne Whillier (Queenston: Edward Mellen Press, 1990), 1.

6. George Grant, *Lament for a Nation* (1965; Ottawa: Carleton University Press, 1970), 24.

7. Transcript, "The Moving Image of Eternity," *Ideas* (Toronto: CBC, 1986), 3.

8. Lamentations, 1:7.

9. Transcript, "Richard Cartwright and the Roots of Canadian Conservatism" (Toronto: CBC, 1985), 25.

10. Grant, *Lament for a Nation*, 65.

11. William Christian, "The Magic of Art," in *By Loving Our Own: George Grant and the Legacy of* Lament for a Nation, ed. Peter C. Emberley (Ottawa: Carleton University Press, 1990), 199.

12. Grant, *Lament for a Nation*, 2.

13. "The Moving Image of Eternity," 5.

14. Grant spent his childhood at Upper Canada College where his father was the headmaster. His maternal grandfather had also been the headmaster there, and was later the secretary of the Rhodes Scholarship Trust and a strong proponent of Imperial Federation, for which he was knighted. His paternal grandfather was the principal of Queen's and "an almost archetypal 'muscular Christian,'" according to Brian McKillop's entry on him in the *Canadian Encyclopedia*. Grant sometimes mocked the idea that his family was especially eminent claiming that his grandfathers were just "two farm boys from the Maritimes who made it in education."

15. Where no reference is given for a quotation from Grant in the remainder of this introduction, it is taken from the text of this interview.

16. Christian, *George Grant*, 152–53.

17. George Grant, *Philosophy in the Mass Age* (Toronto: Copp Clark, 1959), 3.

18. Christian, *George Grant*, 170.

19. Luke 22:42.

20. Grant, *Philosophy in the Mass Age*, 44.

21. Grant, *Philosophy in the Mass Age*, 2nd edition, with a new introduction by George Grant (Toronto: Copp Clark, 1966), vii.

22. Simone Weil, *The Need for Roots* (Boston: Beacon Press, 1952), 253.

23. Grant, *Philosophy in the Mass Age*, 2nd edition, iii.

24. Leo Strauss, *What Is Political Philosophy?* (Glencoe IL: The Free Press, 1959), 55.

25. Hugh Gillis, "Latecomers to the End of History," *The Literary Review of Canada* (March, 1995): 17.

26. Grant, "Tyranny and Wisdom: A Commentary on the Controversy Between Leo Strauss and Alexandre Kojève," *Social Research* 31.1 (Spring 1964): 45–72. Reprinted in

Technology and Empire (Toronto: House of Anansi Press, 1969).

27. This phrase, lately made famous by Francis Fukuyama's 1989 article by that name in *National Interest*, originated with Kojève.

28. Grant, *Lament for a Nation*, 53.

29. Grant, *Technology and Empire* (Toronto: House of Anansi Press, 1969), 89.

30. Grant, *Philosophy in the Mass Age*, 45.

31. Grant, *Time as History* (Toronto: CBC, 1969), 52.

32. Grant, *Lament for a Nation*, 66.

33. I am indebted for insight on this point to Donald Forbes of the Political Science Department of the University of Toronto. His essay on Grant and Strauss will appear in a collection tentatively entitled *George Grant: The Subversion of Technology*, edited by Arthur Davis and forthcoming from University of Toronto Press.

34. Grant, *Technology and Empire*, 132.

35. Grant, "An Ethic of Community," *Social Purpose for Canada*, ed. Michael Oliver (Toronto: University of Toronto Press, 1961), 3–26.

36. Grant, *Lament for a Nation*, 15.

37. See Gad Horowitz, *Canadian Labour in Politics* (Toronto: University of Toronto Press, 1968); and Charles Taylor, *Radical Tories* (Toronto: House of Anansi Press, 1982).

38. See R. K. Crook, "Modernization and Nostalgia, a Note on the Sociology of Pessimism," a review of *Lament for a Nation* in *Queen's Quarterly* 73 (1966): 269–84.

39. "The Moving Image of Eternity," 5.

40. Ibid., 8.

41. The text from which I am quoting was a revised version of the speech published as "A Critique of the New Left" in *Our Generation*, and republished in *Canada and Radical Social Change*, ed. D.I. Rousopolos (Toronto: McClelland and Stewart, 1966), 55–61.

42. David Jay Bercuson and Robert Bothwell, *The Great Brain Robbery: Canada's Universities on the Road to Ruin* (Toronto: McClelland and Stewart, 1984). I heard Grant's comments during a discussion of this book on CBC Radio, but I have not been able to track down the broadcast.

43. Grant, *Technology and Empire*, 77.

44. Grant, *Technology and Justice* (Toronto: House of Anansi Press, 1986), 101.

45. Grant, *Technology and Empire*, 77.

46. Grant, "Sartre," *Architects of Modern Thought* (Toronto: CBC, 1955).

47. Grant, *Philosophy in the Mass Age*, 83.

48. Grant, *Technology and Empire*, 23.

49. George Grant, *English-Speaking Justice* (1974; Toronto: House of Anansi Press, 1975).

50. Grant, *Technology and Empire*, 139.

51. Martin Heidegger, *Basic Writings*, ed. David Farrell Krell (New York: Harper and Row, 1977), 199.

52. T. S. Eliot, *Four Quartets* (New York: Harcourt, Brace and World, 1943), 15.

53. These words conclude many of the canticles in the Anglican Book of Common Prayer.

54. Grant, "Tradition and Revolution," *Revolution and Tradition*, ed. Lionel Rubinoff (Toronto: MacMillan, 1971), 95.

55. Grant, "The Computer Does Not Impose on Us the Way It Should Be Used," in *Beyond Industrial Growth*, ed. Abraham Rotstein (Toronto: University of Toronto Press, 1976), 131.

56. "The Moving Image of Eternity," 10.

57. Grant, *Time as History*, 48.

58. Quoted with no reference given in *Technology and Justice*, 90.

59. Grant, *Time as History*, 45.

60. Grant, *English-Speaking Justice*, 72.

61. Ibid., 74.

62. "Commentary," CBC Radio, March 9, 1988, quoted in *George Grant*, 345.

63. He gave this name, with its echo of national socialism and its indication that Grant was prepared to go to rhetorical extremes on this question, to an early essay on the subject. See *George Grant*, 345.

64. Grant, *English-Speaking Justice*, 92.

65. *The Portable Nietzsche*, ed. Walter Kaufmann (New York: Penguin, 1976).

66. Christian, *George Grant*, 229.

67. Ibid., 228.

68. Simone Weil quotes this saying from the Dao Deh Ching in *The Need for Roots*, 269.

69. Matthew 6:28; Mark 4:28.

70. Matthew 5:45.

71. Weil, *The Need for Roots*, 271.

72. Ibid., 263.

73. Simone Weil, *Waiting for God* (1951; New York: Harper & Row, 1973), 210.

74. Simone Weil, *Gravity and Grace* (London: Routledge & Keegan Paul, 1952), 99.

75. Grant, *Technology and Justice*, 75.

76. Ibid., 75.

77. Weil, *The Need for Roots*, 246.

78. Quoted from *The Will to Power* in *Technology and Justice*, 66.

79. Grant, "In Defence of Simone Weil," *The Idler* 15 (Jan.–Feb. 1988): 40.

80. Grant, *Time as History*, 22.

81. The exact words of the quotations in this sentence are taken from William Christian's précis of an application for sabbatical leave that Grant made in 1956. See *George Grant*, 181.

82. Grant, "In Defence of Simone Weil," 40.

83. Weil, *Waiting for God*, 216.

84. Ibid., 95.

85. Ibid., 97.

86. Grant, "In Defence of Simone Weil," 36.

87. "The Moving Image of Eternity," 5.

88. *By Loving Our Own: George Grant and the Legacy of* Lament for a Nation, 20.

89. "Fyodor Dostoyevsky," in *Architects of Modern Thought*, 3rd and 4th series, CBC Radio, 1959. William Christian reports, in *George Grant*, 178, that this essay was actually drafted by Sheila Grant. "Céline: Art and Politics," *Queen's Quarterly* 90.3 (Autumn 1983): 801–13.

90. Grant, *Technology and Justice*, 39.

91. Christian, *George Grant*, 165.

92. Grant, *Philosophy in the Mass Age*, 81.

93. Grant, *Time as History*, 46.

94. Grant, *Technology and Justice*, 65.

95. The point is made in many places in Charles Taylor's writings, but especially in his 1991 Massey Lectures, *The Malaise of Modernity*, published by House of Anansi Press.

96. Barbara Duden, *Disembodying Women* (Cambridge, MA: Harvard University Press, 1993).

97. In 1939, Grant won a Rhodes scholarship and enrolled in law at Balliol College, Oxford. He was in England when the blitz began.

98. Grant's mother's sister was married to Vincent Massey, who was then Canada's High Commissioner in London.

99. James Doull has since retired and is now Professor Emeritus at Dalhousie.

100. The passage Grant mentions comes from a letter in which Mozart describes how musical ideas come to him. "The idea expands," he says. "I develop it, all becoming clearer and clearer. The piece becomes almost complete in my head, even if it is not a long one, so that afterwards I see it in my spirit all in one look, as one sees a beautiful picture or a beautiful human being. I am saying that in imagination I do not understand the parts one after another, in the order that they ought to follow in the music: I understand them altogether at one moment." Grant quotes this passage in an essay called "Faith and the Multiversity," in his final book, *Technology and Justice*, and cites *Mozart's Briefe*, ed. L. Nohl, 2nd edition, 443–44.

101. The essay was reprinted, along with an addendum written in 1988, in *Two Theological Languages by George Grant and Other Essays in Honour of His Work*, ed. Wayne Whillier (Queenston: Edward Mellen Press, 1990), 6–19. The date of its original composition is given as 1947 in Joan O'Donovan, *George Grant and the Twilight of Justice* (Toronto: University of Toronto Press, 1984), where this essay is discussed on pp. 15–17.

102. An American televangelist with links to the Reagan administration who was prominent at the time the interview was recorded.

103. A Spanish mystic of the sixteenth century, and the author of *Ascent of Mount Carmel* and *Dark Night of the Soul*.

104. A German theologian martyred by the Nazis during World War II.

105. *Philosophy in the Mass Age* was presented as a series of lectures on CBC Radio in 1958 and published in 1959.

106. One of the leaders of the German student movement in 1968.

107. Grant left Dalhousie and returned to Ontario to take up a position at York University in 1960. These events are discussed in Chapter 3.

108. Alexandre Kojève. The Strauss-Kojève controversy was discussed in "Tyranny and Wisdom: A Comment on the Controversy Between Leo Strauss and Alexandre Kojève," reprinted in Grant's *Technology and Empire*.

109. Adler and Hutchins were the editors of *The Great Ideas Today*

1961, which they were preparing under the auspices of the *Encyclopaedia Britannica*. Grant contributed two entries. See William Christian, *George Grant*, 206.

110. Grant is referring to a talk he gave in the CBC's *Architects of Modern Thought* series (CBC, 1955). He contemplated reprinting it in *Technology and Justice*, but did not do so in the end.

111. The group in question was the Student Union for Peace Action (SUPA). Grant's relations with this group are related in more detail in Christian, *Geroge Grant*, 257–60.

112. "An Ethic of Community," 3–26.

113. On February 4, 1963, the minority government of John Diefenbaker was voted out of office when the NDP, which held the balance of power, sided with the Liberals. The vote was prompted by the resignation of Diefenbaker's Defence Minister Douglas Harkness. The issue was whether Canada should accept nuclear warheads for the Bomarc missiles which the Canadian government had already acquired from the United States. In *Lament for a Nation*, published two years later, Grant interpreted these events as the coup de grâce for a sovereign Canada able to pursue a fundamentally different destiny than the United States.

114. Union Nationale Premier of Quebec 1966–1968, and a politician Grant very much admired.

115. The Trudeau government had recently approved testing of Cruise nuclear missiles in Canada.

116. Grant felt that, in the 1980 federal election, Pierre Trudeau had unfairly cast Alberta Premier Peter Lougheed as an enemy of the national interest.

117. This was said at a time when the United States was deeply involved in El Salvador and was actively supporting the overthrow of the Sandanista government in Nicaragua.

118. Grant paraphrased this quotation from memory. I have supplied the actual quotation from *The Portable Nietzsche*, edited and translated by Walter Kaufmann, 432.

119. *The Portable Nietzsche*, 368. Again I have substituted the precise quotation for Grant's paraphrase.

120. Grant is referring to the refusal of medical care to newborns judged incapable of a sufficient "quality of life" to warrant treatment. He treats the question at length in an essay called "The Language of Euthanasia," written with his wife, Sheila Grant, and published in *Technology and Justice*.

121. A point of clarification here: Grant means that God is both present in the world and absent from it; this is the distance between God and God. If God is love and therefore a relation and not a simple substance, then there is a difference and a distance between God and God.

122. Grant called on Mrs. Weil during a visit to France in 1963. See Christian, *George Grant*, 228 ff.

123. Weil, *The Need for Roots*, 242.

124. Matthew 5:45.